The Gourmet's Low Cholesterol Cookbook

Elizabeth S. Weiss
Rita Parsont Wolfson

Henry Regnery Company • Chicago

Library of Congress Cataloging in Publication Data

Weiss, Elizabeth S.
    The gourmet's low cholesterol cookbook.

    1. Cookery for cardiacs. 2. Cholesterol. I. Wolfson, Rita Parsont,
joint author. II. Title.
RM221.C3W45   641.5'63   72-11201

Published by Henry Regnery Company, 114 West Illinois Street
    Chicago, Illinois 60610

Manufactured in the United States of America
Library of Congress Catalog Card Number: 72-11201

For Michael and Stan
with love and thanks

Contents

Acknowledgments

We would like to express our gratitude to the following for their help: The American Heart Association and its helpful and knowledgeable staff, The American Health Foundation, Dr. David Gluck, Mrs. William Parsont, and Mrs. Raymond Schwartz.

Unless Otherwise Stated...

Special margarine refers to liquid vegetable oil margarine (liquid corn or other vegetable oil is the first listed ingredient).

Skim milk refers to commercial skim milk or reconstituted nonfat dry milk.

Canned soup refers to the condensed variety.

Bouillon refers to the canned or homemade varieties, or to those made from cubes or powders.

Flour refers to all-purpose flour.

1

Understanding Cholesterol

This book was inspired, in part, by a patient I cared for while I was serving as an internist in the army.

A fifty-year-old man entered the emergency room complaining of severe pain in his stomach, which had begun abruptly that morning. X rays showed probable evidence of an abdominal aneurysm, a weakening in the wall of the main blood vessel of the abdomen. As the x ray was being read, the patient went into shock. He was rushed to the operating room, and a Dacron graft was inserted in the blood vessel. The patient survived the operation but died two weeks later of complications secondary to the shock and surgery.

Before the sudden onset of his illness this patient had been a vigorous man, with no symptoms of any heart or vascular disease. An aneurysm is usually caused by deposits in the blood vessel, which weaken it and eventually lead to a rupture of the blood vessel wall. Cholesterol is a major component of these deposits. The deposits are formed gradually by a process called atherosclerosis, or hardening of the arteries. Atherosclerosis is the underlying cause of a wide spectrum of heart diseases, aneurysms, and other vascular problems. It is America's number-one killer.

This chapter outlines some of the present information known about the relationship between diet and atherosclerosis. It explains why the American Heart Association, the American College of Cardiology, the Inter-Society Commission for Heart Disease, the American Health Foundation, the Boards of Health of New York and Chicago, and most physicians, nutritionists, and scientists currently recommend a low cholesterol, low saturated fat eating plan for all average healthy Americans.

ATHEROSCLEROSIS

Atherosclerosis is the condition that underlies most heart attacks and strokes. A gradual process, hardening of the arteries begins early in life. Most people have atherosclerosis in a mild form but live a normal life span. Many others die from it.

To understand atherosclerosis, you need to look at the artery. An artery is a tube-like structure through which blood passes from the heart on the way to the vital organs. Artery walls have three layers. Atherosclerosis involves changes in the innermost layer, that layer closest to the blood. For reasons that are not entirely known at present, certain portions of the inner layer may gradually become thickened and roughened by pearly gray deposits of blood, fibrous tissues, a variety of fatty substances, and cholesterol. These bulges diminish the space through which blood may flow and thus make the flow more turbulent. When the deposits prevent sufficient blood from reaching the heart, cardiac pain (angina) and other types of heart disease occur. When an atherosclerotic deposit totally blocks an artery in the heart, a heart attack often results. When a similar process occurs in the brain, the result is usually a stroke. When a deposit forms in other blood vessels in the body, damage to the organ to which the blood is flowing may result.

The American Heart Association gives the grim statistic that more than a million Americans suffer heart attacks each year, which result in more than 675,000 deaths. Approximately 175,000 of these coronary deaths occur in persons under sixty-five years of age. And the death rate is rising. The American Heart Association reports that heart attack fatalities rose by 14 percent for men aged twenty-five to forty-four between 1950 and 1970.

On the average, heart disease kills 1,400 Americans, and cerebral strokes take another 500 lives daily—in total, more than a life a minute. More Americans die of heart attacks than of cancer and accidents combined.

THE CAUSES OF ATHEROSCLEROSIS

The specific causes of atherosclerosis are not fully known at the present time. However, Dr. Thomas Dawber and Dr. William Kannel of the Framingham Heart Study* have demonstrated that excessive fats and cholesterol in the blood, high blood pressure, cigarette smoking, obesity, age, lack of exercise, family history, and stress all seem to increase the chances of a heart attack. Their impressive findings have indicated that there are three major risk factors: excessive fats and cholesterol in the blood (hypercholesterolemia), high blood pressure (hypertension), and cigarette smoking. In this book we are limiting our discussion to the role of fats and cholesterol in the blood.

THE ROLE OF CHOLESTEROL AND FATS IN ATHEROSCLEROSIS

Again, the exact role of cholesterol and fats in atherosclerosis is not completely known. However, we do know that elevated

---

* See chart.

levels of cholesterol in the blood contribute to atherosclerosis.

Atherosclerotic deposits have been produced in almost every species of laboratory animal—dogs, cats, pigs, chickens, ducks, pigeons, guinea pigs, hamsters, and monkeys—by feeding them high-fat, high cholesterol foods. Monkeys have had heart attacks—including sudden fatal ones—similar to those that occur in humans when fed high-fat, high cholesterol foods. These animal studies seem to indicate that diet, even more than stress and other factors, might be a leading cause of heart disease.

In human studies the evidence has also been convincing. Many studies show almost without exception that cholesterol and heart attack rates are lowest in countries in which the diet is low in fats and cholesterol and that rates are highest in nations with high-fat, high cholesterol diets. A recent study comparing middle-aged American and Japanese men showed that the American men had four times as many heart attacks as the Japanese. About 17 percent of the total calories in the American diet were derived from saturated fats, as compared with only 3 percent in the Japanese diet.

Still another study proved the importance of diet by showing that Japanese and other Oriental peoples who immigrated to this country and adopted American eating habits had higher cholesterol levels and a higher coronary related death rate than native Oriental people.

In yet another, ten-year study, a group of middle-aged men in New York formed an Anti-Coronary Club and voluntarily adopted low cholesterol eating habits. In about 30 percent of these men, the blood cholesterol count was reduced to safer levels, and the group heart attack rate was one-fifth the rate expected for this age bracket.

These studies seem to point to the conclusion that reasonable dietary restriction of cholesterol and saturated fat intake is a prudent measure. The American Heart Association maintains that a 15 to 20 percent reduction in cholesterol level among middle-aged men could reduce heart attacks by 25 to 50 percent.

Cholesterol

A man with a blood cholesterol measurement of 250 or above has more than *three* times the risk of one with cholesterol below 194.

Blood Pressure

A man whose blood pressure at systole (the moment the heart contracts) is 151 or higher has *three* times the risk of a man with a systolic blood pressure under 120.

Cigarette Smoking

A man who smokes more than a pack of cigarettes a day has nearly *twice* the risk of a non-smoker.

Average
Heart Attack Risk

These charts show the extent to which particular risk factors raised the risk of heart attack in the male population, aged 30-59, of Framingham, Massachusetts. Columns below the black horizontal line indicate lower than average risk; columns above the line, higher than average risk.

Less than
194

250 and
over

Less than
120

194-220

221-249

151 and
over

250 and over

Non-
Smoker

One
Pack
a Day
or Less

121-130

More
than
One Pack
a Day

131-138

139-150

Source: *The Framingham, Mass., Heart Study — 16 years' experience*

PREVENTION OF HEART DISEASE

Because of the almost epidemic incidence of heart disease in America today, many physicians feel that widespread control is possible only through prevention of severe atherosclerosis. One of the chief preventive measures advocated by most physicians and heart and medical associations is a low cholesterol, low saturated fat way of eating. I avoid using the word "diet" since this often implies a short-term measure. Because atherosclerotic deposits build up gradually over many years, preventing them means a permanent change-over to the low cholesterol, low-fat way of eating.

In discussing any dietary health measure, first and foremost it is necessary to adjust caloric intake to achieve and maintain normal weight. Obesity places an extra burden on the heart, and it increases the risks of high blood pressure, diabetes, and atherosclerotic disease. An obese individual with high blood pressure has five times the risk that a trim individual with normal blood pressure has of developing a heart attack. Since the low fat, low cholesterol way of eating eliminates many fattening foods, it is easier to cut calories. Those who require weight loss, however, should consult a physician.

THE LOW CHOLESTEROL WAY OF EATING

Basically, for the average healthy American without a weight problem, the low cholesterol way of eating calls for the following moderate changes in diet:

1. reduction of dietary cholesterol to less than 300 milligrams per day;
2. reduction of dietary saturated fats;
3. substitution of polyunsaturated fats for saturated fats.

Let us examine each of these.

1. *Reduction of dietary cholesterol to less than 300 milligrams per day*

Cholesterol (from the Greek *cole*, meaning bile, and *steros*, meaning solids) is a waxy substance present in all human beings. We get cholesterol in two ways: it is produced naturally by the body, and it is obtained directly from foods of animal origin that we eat.

Cholesterol is necessary for good health. It performs numerous functions in the body, including acting as a building block for a variety of hormones; helping to transport fatty substances in the bloodstream; and helping to form the insulating material that protects nerve trunks.

However, too much cholesterol can be dangerous. Excess cholesterol may collect in the arteries and other parts of the body. This can lead to an acceleration of the atherosclerotic process, resulting in heart attacks and strokes.

The average American consumes 600 milligrams of cholesterol a day. A number of different studies have shown that reducing this figure to 300 milligrams a day lowers the concentration of cholesterol in the blood of most people.

In order to achieve this recommended reduction, foods containing cholesterol must be limited. Cholesterol is found in the cells of all animals; therefore, it is present in all the animal products we eat—meat, milk, eggs, cheese, etc. Naturally, some animal products have more cholesterol than others. Because cholesterol is produced in the liver in both humans and animals, liver is very high in cholesterol, as are the other organ meats—brain, heart, tongue, etc. Egg yolks are the single greatest source of cholesterol in the average American diet, and they also contain a large amount of saturated fat. (Egg whites do not contain cholesterol or saturated fat.) The typical American breakfast of two eggs, with perhaps a strip or two of bacon, can destroy a low cholesterol eating plan before it gets off the ground.

Unlike animal products, plants contain no cholesterol. Therefore, the consumption of most plant products, such as vegetables, fruits, and grains, does not have to be restricted on a low cholesterol eating plan.

2. Reduction of dietary saturated fats
It has been found that limiting saturated fats is even more effective in lowering blood cholesterol levels than controlling cholesterol consumption. Recent studies of the National Diet

Heart Review Panel of the National Heart Institute, which involved 1,200 men, have shown that the reduction of saturated fat intake and the increase of polyunsaturated fat intake lowers blood cholesterol level even more than does simply limiting cholesterol intake.

It must be stressed that saturated fats are necessary for good health. They are needed by the body to support and protect vital organs, to nourish neurons in the nervous system, and to provide concentrated sources of vitamins A, D, E, and K. Therefore, saturated fats must not be totally eliminated from the diet. However, most Americans eat more than enough fat.

The American Heart Association recommends that fats should comprise 30 to 35 percent of our total caloric intake. This should be broken down to one-third saturated fat, one-third polyunsaturated fat, and one-third monounsaturated fat. In 1970 the average American diet contained 42 percent fat, 36 percent of which was saturated fat. This average figure must be reduced if we are to lower cholesterol levels in the blood.

Saturated fat is found in all meats, as can be seen at a glance. In the United States it is a widespread practice to keep beef cattle relatively stationary in feed lots and feed them heavily. This produces tender meat, but it also produces meat with a high fat content. Since the United States is primarily a country of beef eaters, the high saturated fat content of American diets is easily explained. It is not suggested that we all abstain from eating meat. However, it is wisest to purchase only the leanest meat available and to limit beef, lamb, and pork to three servings a week. (Further information on reducing saturated fat intake and on buying and preparing meat will be found in Chapters 2 and 7.)

Large amounts of saturated animal fat are also found in butter, cream, whole milk, and cheese made from cream and whole milk. These dairy products should be avoided in favor of low fat substitutes.

3. Substitution of polyunsaturated fats for saturated fats
Polyunsaturated fats tend to lower the level of cholesterol

in the blood by helping the body eliminate excess, newly formed cholesterol. Polyunsaturated fats are, simply, fats that are liquid at room temperature. They are chiefly liquid oils of vegetable origin—corn oil, safflower oil, sesame seed oil, soybean oil, sunflower oil, cottonseed oil, and walnut oil.

The American Heart Association recommends reducing saturated fat intake by half while at the same time increasing polyunsaturated fat intake four times. Just increasing poly-unsaturated fat intake without lowering saturated fat intake will not attain the desired results. It might even have the opposite effect, since both fats and calories will be added to the diet.

The polyunsaturated oils are composed chiefly of linoleic acids. Monounsaturated oils, such as olive oil, are composed chiefly of oleic acid and they do not have a cholesterol lowering effect (though they do not raise cholesterol either). Therefore, polyunsaturated oils should be used wherever possible in place of both monounsaturated and saturated fats and oils.

A FAMILY PLAN

A low cholesterol, low saturated fat eating plan is currently being recommended for the entire family by many physicians, nutritionists, and medical societies. Although men have the most heart attacks, this eating plan is an important step toward good health for children and women as well.

Children: One of the most important facts to remember is that atherosclerosis begins early in life. Fatty streaks have been found in the blood vessels of three-year-old children and in the coronary arteries of ten-year-olds. These streaks, though harmless, provide the basis for atherosclerotic deposits, which may accumulate later in life and block blood flow. Heart disease can result.

Many pediatricians are now recommending skim milk for infants and young children of average or above-average weight. This milk contains all the valuable nutrients of whole milk but is lower in fat. How effective a preventive measure this will prove may not be known for years. However, the policy seems to make sense.

Children form eating habits at a very early age, and such habits are often difficult to change. If children become accustomed to low cholesterol, low fat foods, they will form good lifetime eating habits.

Women: The female sex hormone, estrogen, seems for an unknown reason to protect most women from heart disease before menopause. However, after reaching menopause women become as susceptible as men to heart attacks. Many physicians believe that fat and cholesterol deposits in women, as in men, accumulate gradually through the years. In women they become dangerous as soon as menopause occurs. In order to protect themselves in their later years, all women —premenopausal and postmenopausal—should adopt a low cholesterol, low fat eating plan.

Men: A North American man has about one chance in five of developing symptoms of coronary heart disease before the age of sixty. Approximately 25 percent of those experiencing a first premature (before age sixty) heart attack die within three hours of the onset of symptoms. Another 10 percent die within the first week.

A classic atherosclerotic study was done of young men killed in the Korean War. Autopsies showed that nearly eight out of ten men had appreciable atherosclerosis of the coronary arteries. In 10 percent the process had already closed off most of one or more major arteries. It is obviously of prime importance that men switch to a low cholesterol, low fat eating plan.

Most experts believe that mass disease requires mass treatment. Tuberculosis, the late-nineteenth century's number-one killer, was controlled by improved social and sanitary conditions more than by any single drug. Today most experts feel that prevention rather than cure is the way to control heart disease, the twentieth century's number-one killer. While the present evidence is not yet conclusive, most studies seem to point to the validity of a low cholesterol, low saturated fat eating plan for all Americans—men, women, and children —as a means of preventing heart disease.

The following chapters will help you formulate a low cholesterol, low saturated fat eating plan for your family. This plan is intended for healthy people who wish to prevent heart attack and related heart troubles. Those who have high blood pressure, atherosclerosis, or related problems should consult a physician, since they may need a more restricted diet.

Stanley E. Weiss, M.D.
Assistant Director, Renal Unit,
Prospect Heights Division
Long Island College Hospital
Brooklyn, New York

2

The Low Cholesterol Kitchen – a Planning Guide

Once you have become aware of the dangers of eating foods high in cholesterol and saturated fat, you are ready for the next step—conversion to the low cholesterol way of life. This means more than a change in eating habits; you will also have to alter shopping habits and, probably, your methods of preparing foods. However, the rewards for this changeover are ample. Not only will you be contributing to your family's good health and longevity but you will probably find that you are serving tastier meals that are easier to prepare and less expensive.

THE LOW CHOLESTEROL WAY OF LIFE

The average healthy American consumes approximately 600 milligrams of cholesterol a day. It is recommended that

13

healthy Americans, regardless of age or sex, consume no more than 300 milligrams of cholesterol per day, and also reduce intake of saturated fats to about 11 percent of total caloric intake. We believe that the recipes in this book, the discussion of shopping habits, and the methods of food preparation that follow will assist you in lowering your cholesterol and saturated fat intake to acceptable levels.

Of course, overeating, even of healthy foods low in cholesterol and saturated fats, is harmful. No matter how much cholesterol is controlled, overeating and overweight place an extra burden on the heart. This may lead to hardening of the arteries, high blood pressure, strokes, and other heart troubles. Therefore, it is advisable to keep serving size commensurate with age, height, weight, and level of activity.

The foods recommended in this book are widely available in local supermarkets and food stores and should not increase your food budget. Indeed, you might find yourself saving money (many foods high in saturated fats are costly).

BUYER BEWARE

Because so many people have become interested in buying foods low in cholesterol and saturated fat, many of these products are now available. However, some manufacturers, eager to take advantage of this popularity, are marketing products that are not as low in saturated fat as they might seem at first glance. Before you buy any commercially prepared product, be sure to read the label carefully.

For example, we recommend that you use margarine that has liquid corn oil as the first listed ingredient instead of using butter. There are many corn oil margarines on the market today, but a good number of them have hydrogenated corn oil instead of liquid corn oil as the first listed ingredient (ingredients are listed on a product label in order of volume). Since hydrogenated vegetable oil is very high in saturated fat, it will raise cholesterol levels. For the desired cholesterol lowering effect, the oil must be liquid, not hydrogenated.

Another possibly confusing product is low butterfat sour dressing, a nondairy substitute for sour cream. Sour dressings are marketed under a variety of brand names, and some of them are quite tasty. Unfortunately all of them, as far as we can discover, are made with either coconut oil or hydrogenated vegetable oil as the main ingredient, which makes them unacceptable in a low cholesterol eating plan. The labels on these cartons can be misleading; the manufacturer may simply list "vegetable oil" when the ingredient is actually hydrogenated vegetable oil or coconut oil. If you are not sure about what the product contains, call or write to the manufacturer.

A SHOPPING PLAN

Food shopping is the key to low cholesterol cooking. With the right ingredients in the house, you will find you are making low cholesterol, low saturated fat meals almost without trying. Therefore, when you plan your weekly menus and do your food shopping, always select the foods lowest in cholesterol and saturated fats.

In keeping with your family's preferences and caloric limitations, you can buy an unlimited amount of most fruits and vegetables, pastas, and grain products. However, we advise limiting beef, lamb, and pork to three meals a week because these meats are high in saturated fats. Veal is very low in saturated fat and therefore may be eaten frequently. Chicken and other lean poultry are also highly recommended and should be eaten often.

Fish, which is low in cholesterol and contains virtually no saturated fat, should be eaten as often as possible. There has been a good deal of discussion and controversy about the role of shellfish in a low cholesterol eating plan. This is due to the fact that while shellfish has a higher cholesterol content than most meats, it contains no saturated fat. All meats, even the lean ones, contain some saturated fat. Since saturated fat contributes to the build-up of cholesterol in the arteries, the lack of saturated fat in shellfish makes it a desirable food to many doctors and nutritionists. The American Heart Association has recently changed its position from prohibiting the use of shellfish in a low cholesterol eating plan to recommending its limited use.

Of all shellfish, shrimp and crab have the lowest cholesterol content and therefore should be eaten in preference to lobster and oysters. Since a seven-ounce serving of shrimp or crab contains 250 milligrams of cholesterol (and no saturated fat), we recommend that when either of them is served, the cholesterol content of food eaten during the rest of the day be limited to 50 milligrams or less. By counting up cholesterol milligrams in this manner, you can still eat shell-fish, cut down on saturated fat, and stay within the acceptable daily intake of 300 milligrams of cholesterol.

BUYING GUIDE

The buying guide below has been prepared for your con-venience. It lists common foods high in saturated fats and/ or cholesterol, which should be avoided; common foods low in saturated fats and/or high in polyunsaturated fats, which should be purchased; and common foods high in monounsatur-ated fats, which may be purchased in moderation.

Do not buy: foods high in saturated fats and/or cholesterol

As mentioned earlier, excess intake of cholesterol raises the level of cholesterol in the blood; saturated fats also tend to raise the level of cholesterol in the blood. Therefore, foods containing high amounts of cholesterol and saturated fats should be avoided.

Generally, saturated fats are solid at room temperature. All fats of animal origin contain some saturated fat. In addi-tion, some vegetables contain saturated fat. The specific amount of saturated fat found in common foods is listed in the chart beginning on page 146.

The American Heart Association recommends limiting sat-urated fat intake to approximately 11 percent of total caloric intake. For an average twenty-two-year-old man weighing 154 pounds, a daily intake of 2,800 calories is recommended. This would mean a recommended saturated fat intake of 34 grams daily. For an average twenty-two-year-old woman weighing 128 pounds, a daily intake of about 2,000 calories is recommended. This would mean a recommended saturated fat intake of 24.5 grams daily. Since caloric intake should be lessened as we grow older and more sedentary, recommended amounts of saturated fat intake should also decrease accordingly. To help you calculate the amount of saturated fat right for your age, height, weight, and caloric intake recommended by your physician, bear in mind that a gram of saturated fat contains 9 calories.

The following foods are very high in saturated fat and/or cholesterol and therefore should be avoided. Commercial products containing any of these foods should also be restricted.

DAIRY PRODUCTS

Butter

Cream (light, heavy, whipped, half-and-half, and nondairy cream substitutes)

Commercial sour cream and sour cream substitutes

Whole milk (fresh, canned, and powdered; whole milk buttermilk and whole milk yogurt)

Whole milk cheeses

Evaporated or condensed whole milk

Chocolate milk, malted milk, milk shakes, or eggnog

Ice cream

Egg yolks

> Although high in cholesterol, egg yolks contain vitamins, minerals, and protein necessary for good health. Therefore, egg yolks should not be given up completely unless specifically limited by a physician. Most doctors recommend a limit of three egg yolks a week. This figure should include egg yolks consumed in cakes, puddings, etc.

FISH, MEATS, AND POULTRY

Fish:

Lobster

Oysters

Fish roe (including caviar)

Meats:
Bacon, spareribs, and pork sausages
Cold cuts
Fatty beef cuts, such as beef brisket, rib roast, porterhouse,
    and T-bone steak
Fatty cuts of pork
Fatty ground meat
Lamb neck and lamb breast
Organ meats, including brain, liver, kidney, sweetbreads,
    tripe, and giblets
    Since liver is rich in vitamins and iron, it should
    not be completely eliminated from the diet, but
    should be eaten in moderation.
Salt pork
Sausages and frankfurters
Well marbled meats

Poultry:
All poultry fat, including chicken fat
Chicken and other poultry livers
Duck
Goose
Pigeon
    (For a full discussion of fish, meats, and poultry, see
    individual chapters.)

VEGETABLES AND FRUITS

Avocado
Coconut
Olives

FATS AND OILS

Coconut oil
    Of all the oils, coconut oil is the highest in fatty
    acids. Because of its good keeping quality, it is fre-
    quently used in commercially baked goods, candy,
    imitation whipped toppings, and fried or roasted prod-
    ucts such as potato chips and nuts. These products,

of course, should be avoided.

Cocoa butter

Cocoa butter contains the second highest amount of saturated fats in this category. It is the main ingredient of chocolate; therefore, chocolate should be avoided. Cocoa powder is chocolate with much of the cocoa butter removed. Cocoa, which is much lower in saturated fat, is allowed in this eating plan.

Solid and hydrogenated oils

Hydrogenated oils are vegetable oils that have been hardened by a process called *hydrogenation.* This process improves the keeping qualities and some other properties, but it also converts some polyunsaturated fats to monounsaturated and saturated fats. How saturated the fat has become is not always indicated. As a basic guide, these products often contain large amounts of saturated fats: hydrogenated vegetable shortenings, imitation whipped creams, and some margarines.

Palm oil (often used in commercially prepared cookies and pie fillings)

Lard and suet

MISCELLANEOUS

Cake and other commercial baking mixes (except angel food cake)

Chocolate

Commercially prepared baked goods

Custards

Frozen or packaged dinners

Fried or roasted products such as potato chips and popcorn

Hydrogenated peanut butter

Peanuts, cashews, Brazil nuts, and coconuts

Do buy: foods very high in polyunsaturated fats

Polyunsaturated fats tend to lower the level of cholesterol

in the blood by helping the body to eliminate excess, newly formed cholesterol. Generally, polyunsaturated fats are liquid at room temperature. The specific amount of polyunsaturated fats contained in common foods is listed in the chart beginning on page 146. The following foods, high in polyunsaturated fats, are recommended:

Corn oil
Cottonseed oil
Safflower oil
Sesame seed oil
Soybean oil
Sunflower oil
Walnut oil

>(Walnut oil is the most highly polyunsaturated of all the oils, but is not readily available. The next most highly polyunsaturated oil is safflower oil, which is readily available and should be used often.)

Do buy: foods with little or no saturated fat or cholesterol

The specific amount of fats and cholesterol contained in common foods can be found in the chart beginning on page 146. The following foods have little or no saturated fat or cholesterol and therefore are highly recommended. (The foods listed under Fish, Meats, and Poultry may contain moderate amounts of cholesterol and/or saturated fat. However, they are the lowest in saturated fat and cholesterol of the fish, meat, and poultry generally available.)

BREADS AND CEREALS

All breads (white enriched, raisin, English muffins, French bread, Italian bread, oatmeal bread, pumpernickel bread, rye bread, and whole wheat bread)
All cereals (hot and cold)
All pasta except egg noodles
Melba toast and matzohs
Rice

DAIRY PRODUCTS

Curd and low-fat cottage cheese

Egg whites (fresh, frozen, or powdered)

Skim milk and skim milk products (buttermilk made from skim milk, evaporated skim milk, nonfat dry milk, yogurt made from skim milk)

Special margarine

> Not all margarines are low in saturated fat, so be sure to check the label. Those margarines with liquid corn oil or safflower oil as the first listed ingredient are highest in polyunsaturates and should be used.

FISH, MEATS, AND POULTRY

Center cut ham (used in moderation)

Chicken

Fish (all fish, even the so-called "fat" fish)

Lean beef

Lean lamb

Lean pork (used in moderation)

Cornish hen

Shrimp and crab (limiting additional cholesterol intake that day to 50 milligrams)

Turkey

Veal

VEGETABLES AND FRUITS

All green leafy or yellow vegetables

All fruits except avocados and coconuts

BEVERAGES

Beer

Cocoa (made with skim milk)

Coffee

Fruit drinks

Liqueurs

Soft drinks
Tea (with lemon or skim milk)
Whisky (bourbon, Scotch, rye, vodka, rum, etc.)
Wines

MISCELLANEOUS

All dried beans and peas
All spices and herbs
Angel food cake
Bouillon (canned, homemade, or made from cubes
    and powders)
Flour
Gelatin and gelatin desserts
Jelly, jam, marmalade, honey, and molasses
Ketchup, mustard, and vinegar
Marshmallows
Pretzels
Sherbet
Vanilla

Buy in moderation: foods high in monounsaturated fats

Foods high in monounsaturated fats also contain both saturated and polyunsaturated fats but in lower percentages. Monounsaturated fats are usually liquid at room temperature. Unlike saturated fats, monounsaturated fats do not raise the blood cholesterol level. However, unlike polyunsaturated fats, they do not lower it. Therefore, foods in which the monounsaturated fats predominate can be used in moderation. The specific amount of monounsaturated fat contained in common foods is found in the chart beginning on page 146. The following foods are high in monounsaturated fats.

OILS

Olive oil
Peanut oil

Rice oil

> (These oils should be used only on occasions in which their particular taste is necessary to a dish. For general use, we strongly recommend the use of polyunsaturated oils, listed on page 20.)

NUTS

Nuts are the most common food family high in monounsaturated fats, and the following nuts in particular should be used in moderation.

Almonds
Beechnuts
Filberts (hazelnuts)
Hickory nuts
Pecans
Pistachio nuts
Walnuts

> (Of all nuts, walnuts—black and English—contain the highest percentage of polyunsaturated fat and should be used in preference to other nuts when possible.)

The following nuts have a higher percentage of saturated fat and should therefore be avoided.

Brazil nuts
Coconuts (fresh, canned, and dried)
Cashews
Peanuts (raw and roasted)

EQUIPMENT FOR THE LOW CHOLESTEROL KITCHEN

A low cholesterol kitchen does not require any fancy rearranging or expensive new equipment. However, it should have the following basic kitchen equipment:

1. A roasting rack is an absolute *must* since it will enable fats to drip off meats into the bottom of the pan. If the meat roasts in its own drippings, the fat can be reabsorbed.

2. A rib-bottomed skillet helps keep meat from cooking in and absorbing its own fat.
3. The use of a meat thermometer is the only sure-fire way to determine that roasts are cooked to perfection. Since roasting is a recommended method of cooking, a meat thermometer is a wise investment.
4. A large heavy pot or Dutch oven (preferably cast iron, with or without enamel coating) is a boon to any kitchen. Cast iron conducts heat evenly and prevents liquid from boiling away quickly. It also needs less oil or fat for sautéing than does a lighter pot.
5. An earthenware roasting pot is also a good investment. These pots cook poultry, meat, and fish to perfection without the addition of any fat. Follow the manufacturer's directions for use. Never place pot on an open flame.
6. A bulb baster will help you skim fat from gravy and remove fat from roasting pans while cooking.
7. A good set of sharp knives is a *must*, both for trimming away fat before cooking and for carving food later into thin, attractive slices.

FOOD PREPARATION IN THE LOW CHOLESTEROL KITCHEN

The way food—even polyunsaturated and low cholesterol food—is prepared and cooked has a great deal to do with cholesterol and fat intake. Adapting the following methods to daily menu preparation will reduce cholesterol and fat intake.

1. Trim *all* visible fat from all meat and poultry. This is probably the most important rule of all. Place the meat on a large cutting board and, using a large sharp knife, neatly cut away all fat. Ask your butcher to trim your meat before you take it home. You will probably still have to do some additional trimming, but this will save time and effort.
2. Do not overheat polyunsaturated oil until it smokes or burns. Overheating can cause some polyunsaturated fat to turn to saturated fat.

3. Do not deep-fat fry foods. The high temperatures required for deep-fat frying can cause polyunsaturated fats to turn to saturated fats.
4. Remove the skin from poultry after cooking but before serving. Skin is very high in saturated fat.
5. Refrigerate stews, gravies, and stocks overnight. Remove the hardened fat from the top before reheating and serving. Freezing the food will shorten the time needed to harden the fat. If you don't have time for this method, add ice cubes to pan liquids and remove the fat that accumulates on top. Absorb any remaining fat by floating a paper towel or a large lettuce leaf on top for a few moments. Another quick method of removing fat without refrigerating first is to pour gravy or soup into a glass jar or pitcher. After the fat rises to the top, use a bulb baster to remove the liquid gradually from the bottom of the jar.
6. Since the use of egg yolks is limited in this eating plan, we suggest buying powdered or frozen egg whites at your supermarket. This will save both money and time. If you do buy whole eggs, the egg whites can easily be separated from the yolk by cracking the middle of the egg over a bowl with a knife or fork. Transfer the yolk from shell half to shell half, letting the white slip into the bowl beneath.

SAVORY SUBSTITUTES

Savory substitutes are indeed the secret of the low cholesterol gourmet. These substitutes will help you and your family enjoy healthier meals without sacrificing superior taste.

Some substitutes are so close in taste to the original product that it is often impossible to tell the difference. At a recent gathering we served *Charlotte's Chocolate Cake* (page 132). One guest, a strong believer in low cholesterol eating, confessed as he ate the cake, "Chocolate is my only cholesterol vice. I just refuse to give it up. I see you're the same way." When we explained that the chocolate cake was in fact low in cholesterol and saturated fats, he was amazed.

Through our research and kitchen testing, we have found the following substitutes particularly useful:

Polyunsaturated oils instead of saturated or monounsaturated oils

Corn, safflower, and sesame seed oil and other polyunsaturated vegetable oil blends can all be used in sautéing or on salads. Sesame seed oil, with its distinctive flavor, is particularly good for marinating and for a salad oil base. Safflower oil has the lightest taste of these oils and is therefore preferable when substituting for melted shortening in baking or desserts. Olive oil and peanut oil, two monounsaturated oils, can be used when their distinctive taste is necessary to a dish. They do not have a cholesterol lowering effect, so it is recommended that polyunsaturated oils be used in their place whenever possible.

Special margarine (first listed ingredient must be liquid corn or other liquid vegetable oil) instead of butter or solid hydrogenated shortening

Sweet special margarine (first listed ingredient must be liquid corn or other liquid vegetable oil) instead of sweet butter

Evaporated skim milk instead of light cream

Skim milk or reconstituted nonfat dry milk (4 tablespoons powder to 1 cup water) instead of whole milk

Cocoa instead of unsweetened chocolate

Substitute 2½ tablespoons cocoa plus 1½ teaspoons safflower oil for 1 square unsweetened chocolate.

Partially skim milk cheese for whole milk cheese

Partially skim milk cheese is not fat-free and should be used sparingly. However, it should always be used in preference to whole milk cheese. The following partially skimmed cheeses are currently available: partially skimmed cottage cheese, partially skimmed mozarella cheese, neufchatel, partially skimmed Parmesan cheese, partially skimmed ricotta cheese, partially skimmed Swiss cheese.

3

Appetizers

Appetizers should be taste-tempting morsels that whet the appetite. Low cholesterol appetizers are exactly that. They are light, unusual, and delicious, and they are certain to win you compliments. Whether you make Caponata, Tomato Yogurt Cocktail, or any one of the many other low cholesterol appetizers, you can rest assured that they are perfect for serving before dinner, with cocktails, or as snacks.

Do Not Use
  Avocado
  Caviar
  Cream cheese (If a cream-type cheese must be used, substitute Neufchatel. Although it is not a nonfat cheese,

it does contain 33 percent less fat than regular cream cheese.)

Egg yolks

Olives

Sour cream or sour cream substitutes made with coconut or hydrogenated vegetable oil

Do Use

All fresh vegetables

Breads

Curd or low-fat cottage cheese and other low-fat cheeses (see page 26)

Herbs and spices

Ketchup and mustard

Mayonnaise (see page 56)

Skim milk products

Special margarine

Yogurt made from skim milk

Helpful Hints

Since breads are low in cholesterol, keep a loaf of party rye or pumpernickel in the freezer for last-minute guests. Easily defrosted slices can be topped with chopped meats, vegetables, and sauces to make quick, easy, and attractive appetizers.

To make extra-fresh cauliflower and broccoli florets, put the whole cauliflower or broccoli in a bowl of salted ice water for an hour or more; then cut into florets.

Most appetizers can be made ahead of time, covered with plastic wrap, and stored in the refrigerator. If they require baking or broiling, prepare the appetizers up to the cooking point and store them. Cook them at the last minute.

Bagna Cauda

½ cup special margarine (page 21)

¼ cup sesame seed oil

5 garlic cloves, sliced very thin

1½ teaspoon anchovy
paste
Freshly ground black
pepper to taste
Vegetables:
10 cherry tomatoes,
washed

8 small mushrooms,
washed
1 green pepper, seeded
and cut into strips
2 cucumbers, peeled, cut
in half and then verti-
cally into quarters
3 carrots, peeled and cut
in quarters vertically

Combine the margarine and sesame seed oil in a fondue dish.
Cook over low heat until the margarine melts. Add the garlic,
anchovy paste, and pepper. Cook, stirring frequently, until
the mixture is blended, about 2 minutes. Remove fondue dish
to table and serve with vegetables. Serves 6.

Chumus
(Israeli Chickpea Purée)

1 1-pound 4-ounce can
chickpeas, drained
2 medium cloves garlic,
minced
1 teaspoon salt
Dash pepper

1 tablespoon minced
onion
¼ cup fresh lemon juice
1 recipe basic tahina
(page 30)
Minced parsley for
garnish

Place half the chickpeas, 1 clove garlic, ½ tsp salt, dash pepper,
½ tablespoon onion, and 2 tablespoons lemon juice in a blender
container. Process at low speed until mixture is a smooth
purée. Turn into a small bowl and add the remainder of the
chickpeas, garlic, salt, pepper, onion, and lemon juice to the
blender container. Process again until mixture is a smooth
purée; add to the purée already in the bowl. Add the basic
tahina and stir until smooth. Cover tightly with a cover or
aluminum foil and refrigerate at least 3 hours to allow flavors

to blend. Just before serving, sprinkle with parsley. If desired, chumus can be made a day before serving, but be sure that mixture is sealed very tight. If it is exposed to the air, it will dry out.

Serve with pita (Syrian bread), thin crackers, raw vegetables, as a dip. Makes 2⅔ cups.

Tahina

Basic tahina:

½ cup nonhydrogenated unsalted raw sesame butter (or ½ cup sesame seeds processed in blender with 3 table- spoons water until smooth)

3 tablespoons water
2 tablespoons lemon juice
½ tsp salt
1 clove garlic, minced
Pinch chili powder

Mix the sesame butter, water, lemon juice, salt, garlic, and chili powder well. Cover and refrigerate 1 hour to allow flavors to blend. Use as called for in Eggplant Salad (page 34), Chumus (page 29), or other recipes. Makes a generous ½ cup.

Tahina dip:

1 recipe basic tahina
1 tablespoon minced parsley

1 tablespoon fresh lemon juice
2 tablespoons water
2 tablespoons safflower oil

To the basic tahina add the minced parsley, lemon juice, water, and safflower oil. Stir until well mixed. Use as a dip with raw vegetables or serve with pita (Syrian bread). Makes a generous ¾ cup.

Tahina sauce:

1 recipe basic tahina	2 tablespoons lemon juice
1 tablespoon minced parsley	7 tablespoons (½ cup minus 1 tablespoon) water

To the basic tahina add the minced parsley, lemon juice, and water. Stir until well mixed. Serve as a sauce for cooked green vegetables such as broccoli or string beans. Makes about 1 cup.

Banana Orange Juice

3 cups orange juice	¼ banana, peeled and sliced

Put the orange juice and banana slices in a blender container. Process at high speed for 1 minute or until the mixture is completely puréed. Excellent as a brunch appetizer. Serves 4.

Fresh Fruit Cup

16 strawberries, washed and hulled	3 tablespoons orange juice
1 grapefruit, sectioned	1½ bananas, cut into thin slices
3 tablespoons honey	8 mint leaves for garnish

Place a combination of strawberries and grapefruit sections in each of the 4 serving bowls. In a separate container squeeze out all the juice from the grapefruit skins (there should be ½ cup). Add orange juice and honey to grapefruit juice and mix well. To prevent bananas from discoloring, add the banana slices just before serving. Pour the sauce over the fruit and garnish with mint leaves, and serve. Can also be served as a dessert. Serves 4.

Honey Broiled Grapefruit

2 grapefruit
2 tablespoons honey

2 tablespoons blackberry jam

Preheat broiler. Cut grapefruit in half; loosen the sections with a grapefruit knife and remove the seeds. Combine honey and jam. Put 1 tablespoon of honey-jam mixture on top of each grapefruit half. Broil until the grapefruit are browned, about 6 minutes. Serves 4.

Broiled Melon

1 cantaloupe, honeydew melon, or Persian melon

2 tablespoons brown sugar
Juice from 1 lime

Preheat broiler. Cut melon into 1-inch-thick slices. Mix sugar and lime juice and sprinkle over melon slices. Broil until golden, about 5 minutes. Serves 4.

Bombay Stuffed Artichokes

2 large artichokes, 10 to 12 ounces each

1 lemon, cut in half

½ cup fat-free cottage
   cheese
3 tablespoons mayon-
   naise (see page 56)

½ teaspoon curry or
   more, according to
   taste

Trim off artichokes' stems flush with the bases and remove tough leaves at the base. Trim ½ inch off the top of the chokes. With scissors cut the sharp points off leaves. Separate leaves and pull out the center yellow-white leaves in one group. With spoon remove the entire fuzzy, bitter-tasting choke. Squeeze ½ lemon and sprinkle juice over cut portions of artichokes. Put other lemon half in a large kettle of water and bring to a boil. Drop in artichokes. Cook, covered, over low heat for 40 minutes. Drain.

    Combine cottage cheese, mayonnaise, and curry. Stuff artichokes with mixture. Serves 4.

Marinated Artichoke Hearts

⅓ cup sesame seed oil
   Juice of 1 lemon
2 tablespoons parsley,
   minced
1 clove garlic, minced

½ pimiento, seeded and
   minced
1 14-ounce can artichoke
   hearts (use those
   packed in citric juice)

Mix sesame seed oil, lemon juice, parsley, garlic, and pimiento. Marinate artichokes in this mixture in the refrigerator for at least 5 hours. Drain. Garnish each heart with some of the minced pimiento and minced parsley. Serves 4.

Caponata

1 eggplant, about 1½
   pounds

⅓ cup polyunsaturated oil
1 clove garlic, minced

2 cups sliced onion
1 cup chopped celery
1 6-ounce can tomato
   paste
¼ cup water
⅓ cup red wine vinegar
2 tablespoons sugar

2 tablespoons drained
   capers
½ teaspoon salt
¼ teaspoon pepper
½ teaspoon oregano
½ medium green pepper,
   seeded and diced

Wash eggplant and trim off ends but do not peel. Dice into ½-inch cubes.

Heat oil in a Dutch oven or heavy pot. Add eggplant cubes, garlic, onions, and celery. Sauté over high heat for 10 minutes or until onion and eggplant are golden. Add tomato paste and water. Stir well, bring to a boil over high heat, cover, and simmer 15 minutes.

Add wine vinegar, sugar, capers, salt, pepper, oregano, and green pepper. Stir well, cover, and simmer an additional 15 minutes. Let cool; refrigerate (overnight if possible) until ready to serve. Serve cold. Makes 6 cups.

Eggplant Salad

1 eggplant, about 1¼
   pounds
1 recipe basic tahina
   (page 30)
2 tablespoons lemon
   juice
2 tablespoons safflower
   oil

2 tablespoons minced
   onion
2 tablespoons minced
   green pepper
2 tablespoons minced
   parsley
Dash crushed red
   pepper

Peel eggplant and cut off stem end. Slice into ½-inch cubes by cutting eggplant into ½-inch horizontal slices, then cutting vertically at ½-inch intervals. Place eggplant cubes in heavy saucepan with water to cover. Bring to a boil and cook, uncovered, over medium heat 15 to 20 minutes or until very tender. Drain in a colander, turn into a bowl, and mash with a fork.

Add basic tahina, lemon juice, safflower oil, onion, green pepper, parsley, and red pepper. Stir until well mixed. Refrigerate 1 hour or until ready to serve. Serve cold with hot pita (Syrian bread), toast, or thin crackers. Makes about 3¼ cups.

Ratatouille Blanc

½ cup sesame seed oil
1 medium eggplant, about 1½ pounds, cut into small pieces
1 large onion, cut into slices and separated into rings

1 clove garlic, minced
2 tablespoons capers
½ teaspoon oregano
Salt and freshly ground pepper to taste

Pour oil into a Dutch oven. Add eggplant, onion rings, and garlic. Cook, covered, over low heat for 40 minutes or until the eggplant is tender, stirring occasionally. Mix in capers during the last 15 minutes of cooking. Season with oregano, salt, and freshly ground pepper. Chill or serve hot. Serves 4 to 6.

Marinated Mushrooms

¾ cup safflower oil
¼ cup cider vinegar
1 tablespoon lemon juice
¼ teaspoon celery salt
¼ teaspoon dry mustard

1 tablespoon minced parsley
1 teaspoon fennel seeds, bruised
1 clove garlic, minced
1 pound raw mushrooms*

---

* If a cooked mushroom is preferred, poach mushrooms for 5 minutes in 1 tablespoon lemon juice and water to cover before marinating.

Place safflower oil, cider vinegar, lemon juice, celery salt, dry mustard, parsley, fennel seeds, and garlic in a large jar or a bowl that has a cover. Shake until well mixed. Add mushrooms. Cover and shake until mushrooms are coated with marinade. Marinate, covered, for 24 hours in refrigerator, shaking occasionally. Makes about 4 cups.

Tomato Yogurt Cocktail

4 cups tomato juice or V-8 juice	¼ teaspoon prepared white horseradish
2 tablespoons fat-free yogurt	¼ teaspoon sugar
1 teaspoon lemon juice	Salt and freshly ground pepper to taste
¾ teaspoon Worcestershire sauce	¼ teaspoon dill weed

Place all ingredients except dill in blender container. Cover and blend at high speed for 1 minute. Pour into glasses and top each with a sprinkling of dill. Serve immediately. Serves 4 to 6.

Chicken Timbales Hawaiian

1 cup cooked chicken, boned and finely chopped	1 teaspoon parsley, minced
1 whole pimiento, chopped fine	12 pieces fresh spongy white bread, crusts removed and cut into squares ½-inch larger than cup of muffin tin
½ cup crushed pineapple, drained and chopped fine	
2 tablespoons mayonnaise (see page 56)	4 tablespoons special margarine

Preheat oven to 375°F. Mix chicken, pimiento, pineapple, mayonnaise, and fresh parsley. Set aside. Roll bread slices with a rolling pin to flatten. Melt margarine in a small saucepan and brush bread slices on one side with melted margarine. Force bread slices, margarine side down, into muffin tin. Fill with chicken mixture and bake at 375°F. for 10 minutes. Serve immediately (or bread will get soggy). Makes 1 dozen.

4

Soups

Soups are wonderful for the low cholesterol gourmet since everyone loves rich, delicious homemade soup. During the winter, hot soup is the perfect dish to serve to a large group watching TV football games; on a warm summer evening nothing tops the refreshing taste of ice cold soup. And soups are fun to serve. When ladled from a decorative soup tureen, they make truly elegant fare. Best of all, most soups are high in nutrients but very low in saturated fat and cholesterol.

Do Not Use

Commercially prepared canned or frozen soups that contain cream, whole milk, butter, or hydrogenated oil

Cream

Vegetables frozen or canned with butter or cream sauce
Whole milk

Do Use

Bouillon cubes and powders
Commercially prepared bouillon, consomme, beef and chicken broth, and cream soups thickened with nonfat milk, flour, or cornstarch
Skim milk, nonfat dry milk powder, and evaporated skim milk
Tomato and other canned or frozen juices
Vegetables, fresh, frozen, or canned

Helpful Hints

To remove fat from soup or soup stock, chill the soup for several hours. Spoon off hardened fat from the top. For jellied soup, use a knife to loosen stock from the sides of the container and carefully remove the fat. Soups can be placed in the freezer for a few hours to hasten the fat-hardening process.

If you don't have time to refrigerate or freeze the soup, pour it into a glass pitcher. The fat will rise to the top, and the soup can be removed from the bottom of the pitcher with a bulb baster. Another quick removal method is to place some ice cubes in the soup and remove the grease that comes to the top. Float a large lettuce leaf or paper towel on top of the soup to remove any remaining fat. Discard lettuce or toweling and ice cubes.

To make your own creamed soups, try using evaporated skim milk or skim milk mixed with nonfat dry milk powder instead of cream. Reconstitute dry milk with warm water for best results.

If you are cooking fresh vegetables in water, use the vegetable liquid as part of the water requirement when making soup. This assures extra vitamins and minerals and adds flavor.

Burmese Soup

4 cups chicken broth
½ teaspoon celery flakes
1 carrot, peeled and
finely chopped
1 onion, finely chopped
½ to ¾ teaspoon curry,
according to taste

½ banana, peeled and
puréed or thoroughly
mashed
2 tablespoons lemon
juice
½ cup evaporated skim
milk

Combine all ingredients except evaporated skim milk in a saucepan. Bring to a boil and simmer, uncovered, for 10 minutes. Cool. Add the evaporated skim milk and simmer over very low heat until heated through. (Do not boil.) Serves 4.

Chicken Gumbo

3 tablespoons polyunsat-
urated oil
1 3-pound frying chick-
en (all visible fat re-
moved), cut up
2 medium onions,
chopped
7 cups water
1½ teaspoons salt
1 bay leaf
1 stalk celery, chopped
1 8-ounce can tomatoes

1 10-ounce package fro-
zen whole kernel corn
1 10-ounce package fro-
zen cut okra
¼ cup raw rice
⅓ cup green pepper,
seeded and chopped
1 teaspoon paprika
Freshly ground black
pepper to taste
Dash crushed red
pepper

Heat oil in the bottom of a soup kettle or Dutch oven. Add chicken pieces and onion and sauté until the chicken is lightly browned on all sides and the onion is translucent. Add water, salt, bay leaf, and celery. Drain tomatoes and add the liquid to the kettle. Bring to a boil, cover, and simmer

1½ hours or until chicken is tender and ready to fall off the bone. Remove chicken and refrigerate. Skim fat from broth (or refrigerate at this point until fat hardens and can be removed easily).

Reheat refrigerated broth and add tomatoes, corn and okra just as they come from the carton, and rice. Bring to a boil, stirring occasionally, and simmer, covered, over low heat for 20 minutes. When chicken is cool enough to handle, remove meat from bones and cut into small cubes. Discard bones and skin. Add chicken cubes, green pepper, paprika, black pepper, and crushed red pepper to the simmering broth. Taste to see if more salt is needed. Simmer an additional 10 minutes before serving.

This soup makes a hearty main dish. Serve with a green salad and crackers or bread. If you serve the soup as a first course instead of a main dish, use only half the chicken cubes in the soup. Reserve the rest of the chicken for salad. Makes 10 cups.

Cream of Mushroom Soup

3 tablespoons special margarine (page 21)
1 medium onion, chopped
2 cups fresh mushrooms, sliced
3 cups water
3 beef bouillon cubes
½ cup evaporated skim milk
Dill for garnish

Melt margarine in the bottom of a large kettle. Add onion and mushrooms. Cook, stirring, until onions are transparent and mushrooms are tender (6 to 8 minutes). Add water and bouillon cubes and bring mixture to a boil. Reduce heat and simmer for 5 minutes. Remove from heat and cool. Add evaporated skim milk. Simmer over very low heat for 2 minutes (do not boil). Serve garnished with dill. Serves 4.

Cream of Tomato Soup

2 large tomatoes, peeled*
  and chopped
1 onion, sliced
2 tablespoons tomato
  paste
1½ cups chicken broth

1 bay leaf
  Salt and freshly ground
  pepper to taste
¾ cup evaporated skim
  milk
  Basil for garnish

Combine chopped tomatoes, onion slices, tomato paste, chicken broth, and bay leaf in a saucepan. Bring to a boil and simmer, uncovered, for 5 minutes. Cool. Season with salt and pepper. Pour into blender container and blend until well mixed. Add evaporated skim milk. Reheat in saucepan. Simmer, uncovered, until heated through. Do not boil. Serve garnished with basil. Serves 4.

Gazpacho

3 cups tomato juice,
  chilled
½ cup chicken broth
1 tomato, peeled and
  chopped
½ cucumber, peeled and
  chopped
½ green pepper, seeded
  and chopped
1 scallion, chopped
1 tablespoon polyunsat-
  urated oil
1 tablespoon wine
  vinegar

  Dash Tabasco
1 tablespoon lemon juice
½ apple, peeled and
  chopped
1 piece white bread,
  crusts removed
1 clove garlic, minced
  Salt and freshly ground
  pepper to taste

Garnish:
½ green pepper, seeded
  and chopped

---

* To remove skin from tomatoes, immerse tomatoes in boiling water for 30 seconds. Then peel skin with a sharp knife.

½ cucumber, peeled and
chopped
½ apple, chopped

½ cup garlic croutons
½ onion, minced

Place all soup ingredients in a blender container. Blend until all ingredients are well mixed. Put each of the garnishes in a separate bowl. Serve soup well chilled and have guests garnish their own serving to taste. Serves 4 to 6.

Mandarin Watercress Soup

3 cups chicken broth
1½ cups bottled clam juice
2 scallions, sliced
diagonally

1 large tomato, peeled*
and chopped
½ bunch watercress
1 teaspoon sesame seed
oil

Place chicken broth, clam juice, and scallions in a large saucepan. Add chopped tomato to broth mixture. Bring mixture to a boil and simmer 1 minute. Add watercress and simmer 1 more minute. Just before serving add sesame seed oil. Serves 3 to 4.

Old-Fashioned Chicken Soup

1½ pounds chicken backs
and necks (all visible
fat removed)
10 cups water
1 teaspoon salt
¼ teaspoon poultry
seasoning

¼ teaspoon pepper
2 stalks celery, including
leaves, sliced
2 carrots, peeled and
sliced
1 onion, quartered
2 sprigs parsley

---

* To remove skin from tomatoes, immerse tomatoes in boiling water for 30 seconds. Then peel skin with a sharp knife.

Place all ingredients in a heavy pot or Dutch oven. Bring to a boil, cover, and simmer gently for 2 hours. Meat can be removed from bones and served in soup or used for salad. Discard celery leaves and parsley sprigs before serving. Makes 6 to 7 cups.

Vichyssoise

2 tablespoons special
 margarine (page 21)
½ cup leeks (white part
 only), sliced
1 medium onion, sliced
4 medium potatoes,
 peeled and sliced

6 cups chicken broth
½ cup skim milk
½ cup evaporated skim
 milk
 Chopped chives for
 garnish

Melt margarine in a large kettle. Add leeks and onion and sauté until onion is transparent. (Do not let mixture get too brown.) Add potatoes and broth and cook, partially covered (with the lid slightly ajar), for 40 minutes or until the potatoes are very tender. Cool. Pour half the mixture into a blender container. Hold the top very firmly (warm mixtures cause increased pressure inside the container) and blend at high speed until mixture is puréed. Pour into a large bowl. Pour the other half of the mixture into the blender container and process at high speed until puréed. Add mixture to the large bowl. Stir in skim milk and evaporated skim milk. Chill thoroughly. Before serving process in blender at high speed for 1 minute. Serve garnished with chopped chives. Serves 6.

5

Salads and Salad Dressings

Salad is a marvelous addition to any meal. A great variety of salads—including mixed green salads, vegetable salads, aspics, and fruit salads—can be used in your low cholesterol meals. Many are hearty enough to use as main dishes, particularly during the summer.

Do Not Use
Avocados
Commercial bottled salad dressings that contain cheese or hydrogenated oil
Egg yolks
Olive and peanut oil (may be used sparingly)
Olives

Vegetables with butter or sauces added
Whole milk cheeses

Do Use
  All fruit, fresh, frozen, or canned (except avocados)
  All gelatins
  All herbs and spices
  All vegetables, fresh, frozen, or canned, except those with
    butter or sauces added
  Commercial salad dressings made with polyunsaturated
    vegetable oils
  Ketchup
  Mayonnaise
  Plain and flavored vinegar
  Polyunsaturated oils

Helpful Hints
  Since heat can wilt fresh vegetables, chill your salad bowl, salad servers, and individual bowls or plates for an hour or two before serving. In order to keep greens crisp and fresh, dry them thoroughly, piece by piece, until absolutely water-free.
  To keep perishable vegetables (such as parsley) fresh in your refrigerator, wrap them in a damp paper towel and store them in a plastic bag in crisper.
  Salad dressing can be kept in a covered jar in the refrigerator, but it should not be kept much longer than a week. Most dressings taste best when they are made fresh for each salad.
  When using salad dressing, pour on a little at a time. Too much dressing causes a salad to get soggy.
  Salad greens should not be cut with a knife. Tear them gently by hand into bite-sized pieces.
  Leftover drained vegetables—green beans, cauliflower, artichokes, carrots, peas, etc.—can be added to a green salad with good effect.
  To mince parsley quickly, use a pair of scissors, a large knife, or a cleaver.

Cucumber Aspic

2 cups cucumber, peeled and diced (1 large cucumber)
1 tablespoon chopped onion
1 tablespoon lemon juice
½ cup chicken bouillon
1 3-ounce package lemon gelatin
¼ teaspoon salt
½ cup boiling water
¼ cup celery, chopped fine
1 carrot, peeled and grated
2 tablespoons minced parsley

Place cucumber, onion, lemon juice, and bouillon in a blender container. Process at medium speed until puréed. Set aside.

Soften gelatin and salt in boiling water. Stir over low heat until dissolved. Stir gelatin mixture into cucumber purée. Stir in the celery, carrot, and parsley and pour into a 3-cup mold. Chill until firm. Unmold on lettuce leaves if desired. Serves 4.

Pineapple Crunch

1 cup low-fat cottage cheese
1 tablespoon skim milk
1 8¼-ounce can crushed pineapple and syrup
1 tablespoon lemon juice
½ cup minced celery
1 carrot, peeled and grated
⅔ cup water
1 ¼-ounce envelope unflavored gelatin (1 tablespoon)
½ cup boiling water

Beat cottage cheese and milk together with an electric mixer until smooth. Stir in pineapple and syrup, lemon juice, celery, carrot, and ⅔ cup water.

Soften gelatin in the boiling water. If necessary, cook over low heat until dissolved. Pour gelatin mixture into pineapple-cottage cheese mixture. Stir well and pour into a

3- or 4-cup mold. Chill until firm. Unmold on lettuce leaves if desired. Serves 4.

Tomato Aspic

1 ¼-ounce envelope (1 tablespoon) unflavored gelatin	1 tablespoon minced onion
2 cups V-8 or Vegemato juice	3 tablespoons celery, finely chopped
1 tablespoon lemon juice	1 cup cabbage,finely shredded
1 teaspoon sugar	⅓ cup apple, peeled, cored, and chopped
¼ teaspoon salt	

Soften gelatin in half a cup of V-8 or Vegemato juice in a saucepan. Cook, stirring, over low heat until gelatin is dissolved. Turn into a 3- or 4-cup mold and stir in the remaining 1½ cups juice, lemon juice, sugar, and salt. Chill until slightly thickened. Stir in onion, celery, cabbage, and apple. Chill until firm. Unmold on lettuce leaves if desired. Serves 4.

Beet Salad

1 1-pound can sliced beets, drained	2 cloves
½ red onion, cut into thin slices and broken into rings	⅓ cup white vinegar
	2 tablespoons water
	2 teaspoons sugar
	1 bay leaf

Put beets and onion rings in a large bowl. Combine cloves, vinegar, water, sugar, and bay leaf. Pour over beets and onion rings. Refrigerate and marinate 2 hours or more. Serves 4.

Chinese Salad

1 cucumber, unpeeled
  and sliced thin
1 carrot, peeled and
  shredded
2 scallions, chopped
  (optional)

2 tablespoons soy sauce
2 tablespoons sesame
  seed oil
1 tablespoon white
  vinegar
¼ teaspoon sugar

Put cucumber slices, shredded carrot, and chopped scallions in a salad bowl. Combine soy sauce, sesame seed oil, vinegar, and sugar. Pour over the cucumber mixture and toss gently. Serves 4.

Cucumbers Scandia

2 firm cucumbers
1 small yellow onion,
  sliced paper thin and
  separated into rings
¼ cup cider vinegar
2 tablespoons water

1 tablespoon sugar
¼ teaspoon dry mustard
  Salt and freshly ground
  black pepper to taste
1 tablespoon minced
  parsley

Pare cucumbers and slice very thin. Squeeze gently to remove some of the excess moisture and pat dry with a paper towel. Place in a bowl with the onion rings. In a separate bowl mix cider vinegar, water, sugar, dry mustard, salt, pepper, and parsley. Pour over cucumber and onions and mix well. Chill at least 1 hour. Serves 4.

Marinated Green Beans

1 9-ounce package frozen
  French-style green
  beans

3 tablespoons polyunsat-
  urated oil

2 tablespoons wine
   vinegar
¼ teaspoon dry mustard
½ teaspoon oregano
½ teaspoon salt
¼ teaspoon pepper

½ sweet pimiento, seeded
   and chopped
1 tablespoon minced
   onion
1 tablespoon minced
   parsley

Cook beans according to package directions. Drain and set aside.

Mix well oil, vinegar, dry mustard, oregano, salt, and pepper. Add beans, pimiento, onion, and parsley. Toss gently until all is coated with dressing. Chill at least 2 hours in refrigerator to allow flavors to blend. Serves 3.

Marinated Summer Salad

1 cucumber, peeled and
   sliced very thin
8 cherry tomatoes,
   halved
1 green pepper, seeded
   and sliced

1 tablespoon sesame seed
   oil
1 tablespoon white
   vinegar
1 tablespoon lemon juice
¼ teaspoon tarragon

Place cucumber slices, cherry tomatoes, and green pepper slices in a bowl. Mix sesame seed oil, vinegar, and lemon juice. Pour over salad. Sprinkle with tarragon. Cover and refrigerate 2 hours or more. Serves 4.

Potato Salad

2 pounds new potatoes
1 tablespoon dry white
   wine

½ cucumber, scored with
   a fork, sliced thick and
   quartered

3 tablespoons safflower
  oil
1 tablespoon wine
  vinegar

1 tablespoon shallots,
  minced
1 teaspoon parsley flakes
  Salt and freshly ground
  pepper to taste

Put potatoes in a large kettle of water. Cook over medium heat 20 minutes or until potatoes are tender. Drain, peel, and cut each potato into quarters. Add white wine while the potatoes are still warm. Add cucumber quarters. Pour safflower oil, wine vinegar, shallots, and parsley flakes over all. Season with salt and freshly ground pepper. Serves 4 to 5.

Spicy Cole Slaw

6 cups shredded cabbage
1 small onion, grated
1 carrot, peeled and
  grated
1 tablespoon minced
  parsley
¼ cup safflower oil
3 tablespoons cider
  vinegar

¼ cup mayonnaise (see
  page 56)
1 tablespoon sugar
¼ teaspoon dry mustard
⅛ teaspoon garlic powder
½ teaspoon celery seed
  Salt and freshly ground
  black pepper to taste

Toss cabbage, onion, carrot, and parsley until well mixed.

Mix well safflower oil, cider vinegar, mayonnaise, sugar, dry mustard, garlic powder, celery seed, salt, and pepper in a small bowl. Pour over cabbage mixture and toss gently until well mixed. Chill at least 2 hours to allow flavors to blend. Serves 6.

Spinach Salad

1 pound spinach

½ pound mushrooms,
  sliced

12 cherry tomatoes,   Juice of 1 lemon
      halved   1 clove garlic, peeled
 2 scallions, chopped   Salt and freshly ground
 ⅓ cup sesame seed oil   pepper to taste

Tear stems off spinach, wash well, and drain. Tear spinach into bite-sized pieces. Place in a salad bowl and add mushrooms, tomatoes, and scallions. Cover with a damp, clean cloth and refrigerate. Combine oil, lemon juice, garlic, salt, and pepper, in a container and refrigerate. When ready to serve, discard garlic and pour dressing over spinach salad. Toss lightly and serve. This makes a very attractive salad for buffet or family-style serving. Serves 6.

Watercress Salad

 ¼ cup safflower oil   2 bunches watercress,
 2 tablespoons wine   washed in ice cold
      vinegar   water
 ¾ teaspoon parsley flakes   10 cherry tomatoes,
 1 clove garlic   halved

Combine oil, wine vinegar, parsley flakes, and garlic. Refrigerate 2 hours or more to allow flavors to blend.
   Cut off bottom part of watercress stems to make short sprays. Combine watercress with halved tomatoes. Just before serving, discard the garlic, pour dressing over salad, and toss lightly. Serves 4.

Zucchini Salad

 4 zucchini, washed and   1½ cups chicken bouillon
      sliced   ⅛ teaspoon salt

3 tablespoons sesame
  seed oil
Juice of 1 lemon
1 clove garlic, minced

12 cherry tomatoes,
  halved
1 teaspoon dried onion,
  minced
½ teaspoon tarragon

Combine zucchini, chicken bouillon, and salt in a saucepan. Cover and bring to a boil. Reduce heat and simmer 8 to 10 minutes or until zucchini is crisp but tender. (If you overcook, the zucchini will be mushy.) Drain and refrigerate.

Mix sesame seed oil, lemon juice, and garlic in a small bowl. Cover and refrigerate until ready to serve. Just before serving, put zucchini slices and tomatoes in a large bowl, pour over the dressing, sprinkle with minced onion and tarragon, and toss lightly. Serves 6.

Dutch Salad Dressing

¼ cup sesame seed oil
2 tablespoons white
  vinegar

2 tablespoons ketchup
1 teaspoon basil
⅛ teaspoon salt
Pepper to taste

Combine all ingredients and shake well. Serve over tossed green salad. Makes ½ cup.

French Dressing

3 tablespoons red wine
  vinegar
2 tablespoons lemon
  juice
½ teaspoon paprika
½ teaspoon salt

¾ teaspoon dry mustard
½ teaspoon sugar
  (optional)
¼ teaspoon black pepper
1 small clove garlic
½ cup polyunsaturated
  oil

Combine all ingredients in a screw-top jar and shake well. Let stand in refrigerator 1 hour. Remove garlic and shake well before serving. Makes ¾ cup.

Honey Lime Dressing

Juice of 1 lime
2 tablespoons honey
2 tablespoons safflower
  oil

2 tablespoons orange
  juice
¼ teaspoon celery seed

Combine all the ingredients and mix well. Serve on any fruit salad. Makes ½ cup.

Italian Salad Dressing

2 tablespoons wine
  vinegar
¼ cup polyunsaturated
  oil

1 clove garlic
¼ teaspoon oregano
¼ teaspoon paprika
  Salt and freshly ground
  pepper to taste

Shake all ingredients together in a jar. Refrigerate 2 hours or more to allow flavors to blend. Before serving, remove the whole garlic. Serve over tossed green salad. Makes ⅓ cup.

Mayonnaise

1 whole egg
¾ teaspoon dry mustard
½ teaspoon salt

3 drops Tabasco sauce
½ teaspoon sugar

2 tablespoons lemon
  juice
1½ to 1¾ cups safflower oil

½ teaspoon prepared
  brown mustard

Place egg, dry mustard, salt, Tabasco sauce, and sugar in
a blender container. Cover and blend at high speed for 40
seconds. Add 1 tablespoon lemon juice and blend another
10 seconds. Measure out ¾ cup safflower oil. While blending
at high speed, add oil by drops to egg mixture. (If blender
container is uncovered when oil is added, a good deal of
spattering will result. If a small funnel is available, uncover
a tiny corner of blender container, put funnel in, and add
oil through funnel.) Stop processing at occasional intervals
and push mixture toward blades with a spatula.

When ¾ cup oil has been added, the mixture should be
thick and fluffy. Pour into bowl. Beat at high speed with
an electric mixer, adding an additional ¾ to 1 cup oil in a
slow stream. The amount of oil depends on how much the
egg will absorb. Stop adding oil when oil merely floats on
top of mixture and does not become mixed. Beat in remaining
tablespoon of lemon juice and the brown mustard. Put mayonnaise into an air-tight jar and refrigerate until needed.
Makes 1½ to 1¾ cups.

NOTE: The two-step process, from blender to mixer, insures
a thick, failure-proof mayonnaise. If made totally in blender,
a thinner mayonnaise will result. If made only in a mixer,
inexperienced cooks may end up with a mixture that fails
to emulsify.

Thyme Dressing

¼ cup sesame seed oil
  Juice from 1 lemon

¼ teaspoon sesame seeds
¼ teaspoon thyme
1 clove garlic

Combine all ingredients and mix well. Refrigerate for 2

hours or more to allow seasonings to blend. Before serving, discard garlic. Serve over tossed green salad. Makes ½ cup.

Vinaigrette Sauce

¼ cup polyunsaturated
  oil
1 tablespoon lemon juice
1 tablespoon tarragon
  vinegar
½ teaspoon salt
¼ teaspoon pepper

½ teaspoon prepared
  brown mustard
1 teaspoon drained
  capers, minced
1 teaspoon minced
  parsley
1 teaspoon minced onion
  or scallion

Combine ingredients in a screw-top jar. Shake until well mixed. Use on asparagus or cold roast beef. Makes a generous ⅓ cup.

6
Meats

Since most of our cholesterol intake comes from animal products, the proper selection and preparation of meat is particularly important. In deciding which meats to buy, remember that grade does not indicate fat content. Prime or choice grades used to be highest in fat content, but this is no longer true. However, they are still not necessarily the leanest. For cholesterol watchers it is extremely important to use only the leanest meat and to trim all visible fat from all meats.

Even the leanest cuts of beef, pork, and lamb are higher in saturated fat than poultry, fish, or veal. Therefore, it is recommended that beef, pork, and lamb be limited to three meals a week.

Do Not Use

Bacon (except Canadian bacon)

Brisket, rib roast, and other fatty cuts of beef

Commercial gravies

Frankfurters and sausages

Liver, brain, heart, kidney, and other organ meats. (Because of its high vitamin and mineral content, liver should be served about once a month, not totally eliminated from the diet)

Luncheon meats

Prepackaged ground meat

Salt pork

Spareribs

Well-marbled meat (meats in which you can see a large amount of fat throughout)

Do Use

Different lean cuts of meat have varying amounts of fat content and therefore can make a great difference in your cholesterol intake. For example, one **ounce of lean roasted top round** contains a bit over one gram of fat, while one ounce of lean roasted ribs of beef contains about four grams of fat.

It is impossible to present a complete list of all the lean cuts of meat since even the same cuts vary a great deal in fat content. However, as a general rule, try to buy the cuts listed below.

Beef: Sirloin roast, top round, eye round, bottom round, silvertip roast, or rump roast for roast beef

Round or very lean chuck for stew

Lower round corned beef (instead of brisket corned beef)

Ham: Can be used sparingly. Center cut is the leanest portion.

Lamb: Leg of lamb is generally the leanest cut. Trim well before roasting. Leg of lamb can also be cut up for stew and should be used in preference to shanks, breast, or neck meat. Well-trimmed lamb shoulder is also good for stews.

Pork: Well-trimmed chops are usually the leanest cuts.

Veal: Of all meats, veal is usually lowest in saturated fats and should be used often. Best cuts are scallops, leg, or shoulder. Breast is usually fatty.

Helpful Hints

Trim all visible fat from all meats. This is essential in reducing cholesterol intake. Place meat on a wooden cutting board and cut away fat with a very sharp knife. Remember, even if you ask your butcher to trim meat, you will still have to do some trimming yourself.

Do not buy prepackaged ground meat; it contains large amounts of fat. Pick out a lean piece of meat and ask the butcher to trim it well before grinding it.

Instead of basting meat with its own drippings, baste with wine, tomato juice, or bouillon.

Remove excess liquid fat from cooked lamb chops, pork chops, and steak by blotting the meat with paper towels before serving.

Use less meat per serving. Casseroles, stews, and meat dishes served over rice or pasta stretch the amount of meat needed per serving. (Your food budget will also benefit.)

Broil rather than pan-fry steaks, lamb chops, and hamburgers.

Always roast meat on a rack so that it does not sit in its own fat. Pour off fat from pan or remove with a bulb baster while meat is roasting if vegetables are cooking in the bottom of the pan.

Beef for stew will be leaner—and more economical—if you buy a whole piece of meat and cut it up yourself after trimming it. Bottom or top round or a lean piece of chuck are good cuts of meat for stew.

To keep steak or lamb chops from curling when broiling, make diagonal slashes along the edges of the meat after trimming off all visible fat.

Always Perfect Roast Beef

1 6-pound eye of round*,
trimmed of visible fat
Garlic salt to taste (or
2 cloves garlic, slivered
and inserted in roast)

Salt and freshly ground
pepper to taste
1 large onion, cut into
slices

Preheat oven to 325°F. Wipe roast with a damp cloth. Put the roast, fat side up, on a roasting rack in a shallow roasting pan. Sprinkle with garlic salt, salt, and freshly ground pepper. Fasten the onion slices to the top of the roast with toothpicks. Put any remaining slices in the bottom of the pan. Leave the seasoned meat at room temperature for one hour before roasting.

Insert a meat thermometer into the thickest part of the roast. Cook until the thermometer registers 140°F. for rare (32 minutes per pound), 150°F. for medium rare (35 minutes per pound), 160° F. for medium (38 minutes per pound), or 170°F. for well done (48 minutes per pound). Serves 12.

Beef Roast Chinois

2 tablespoons soy sauce
1 tablespoon sesame seed
oil
½ tablespoon dry
mustard
2 tablespoons honey
1 clove garlic, minced

½ teaspoon powdered
ginger
1 onion, sliced
3 pounds top or bottom
round or other lean
beef (all visible fat
removed)
1 1-pound can chop suey
vegetables, drained

Mix soy sauce, sesame seed oil, dry mustard, honey, garlic, and ginger thoroughly. Add onion and meat. Turn meat

---

* If you wish to make a smaller roast beef, use a 2- to 3-pound silvertip roast or a 3- to 4-pound sirloin roast. Proceed as directed above.

several times until it is completely coated with soy sauce mixture. Cover and marinate in the refrigerator for 2 hours, turning occasionally.

Preheat oven to 350°F. Place meat, onions, and marinade in a Dutch oven. Cover and bake at 350°F. for 1 hour. Add drained chop suey vegetables, cover, and bake 40 minutes more or until meat is tender. Serves 6.

Beef Teriyaki

1½ pounds lean beef (shell, sirloin, or flank steak)
¼ cup sherry
¼ cup soy sauce
½ lemon, thinly sliced
1 clove garlic, mashed
3 tablespoons sugar
½ small apple, grated fine

Trim all visible fat from the meat and cut into thin strips. Combine sherry, soy sauce, lemon slices, garlic, sugar, and grated apple. Marinate meat in mixture for 3 hours in refrigerator. Drain. Cook meat quickly on each side in a heavy skillet over moderate heat. Serves 4.

Caraway Beef Stew

3 tablespoons polyunsaturated oil
3 pounds top or bottom round or other lean beef (all visible fat removed), cut into 2-inch cubes
4 onions, coarsely chopped
1 clove garlic, minced
1 teaspoon salt
½ teaspoon freshly ground pepper
1 8-ounce can tomato sauce
1 tablespoon caraway seeds
1 teaspoon thyme

4 carrots, peeled and sliced	½ green pepper, seeded and cut in julienne strips
	½ teaspoon basil

Heat oil in a Dutch oven or heavy pot. Add beef cubes, onion, and garlic and sauté until beef is lightly browned on all sides and onion is golden. Stir in salt, pepper, tomato sauce, caraway seeds, and thyme. Bring to a boil, cover, and simmer over low heat for 1 hour. Add carrots and simmer 30 minutes more. Stir in green pepper strips and basil. Mix well, cover, and simmer an additional 10 minutes or until all vegetables are tender. Serve over rice if desired. Serves 6.

Cherry Flank Steak

1 2-pound flank steak (all visible fat removed), scored on both sides	1 tablespoon vegetable oil
Meat tenderizer	1 apple, cored and diced
2 tablespoons lemon juice	1 10-ounce package frozen cherries, defrosted

Sprinkle meat on both sides with meat tenderizer. Pour on lemon juice and let meat marinate at room temperature for 2 hours. Heat vegetable oil in a large skillet. Brown the meat on both sides. Add diced apple and frozen cherries with their juice. Cover, reduce heat, and cook for 25 to 30 minutes or to desired degree of doneness. To serve, cut meat into 1-inch slices and pour cherry-apple mixture over the meat. Serves 4.

Prebonata (Corsican Beef Stew)

Stew:	beef (all visible fat removed), cut into ¾-inch cubes
3 pounds top or bottom round or other lean	

1 teaspoon salt
¼ teaspoon pepper
3 tablespoons flour
2 tablespoons polyunsat-
  urated oil
2 cloves garlic, minced
1 bay leaf
½ cup beef stock
¼ cup parsley, chopped
  fine
  Tomato base:
1 1-pound 1-ounce can
  tomatoes

2 teaspoons juniper
  berries
2 onions, chopped
2 tablespoons parsley,
  finely chopped
1 green pepper, seeded
  and cut in julienne
  strips
½ pimiento, seeded and
  cut in julienne strips

Season beef cubes with salt and pepper and place in a paper bag. Add flour and shake bag until beef cubes are coated evenly. Heat oil in a heavy pot or Dutch oven. Add beef cubes and garlic and sauté until beef is lightly browned. Add bay leaf and beef stock. Bring to a boil. Cover and simmer 1½ hours or until tender. Stir often and check liquid frequently. If it seems to be boiling out, add more stock, a few tablespoons at a time. There should be very little gravy at the end of the cooking time. When beef is tender, add parsley and simmer 5 more minutes.

While beef is cooking, combine the tomatoes and their liquid, juniper berries, and chopped onion in a heavy skillet. Bring to a boil and simmer, uncovered, over low heat for 20 minutes. Add parsley, green pepper, and pimiento. Simmer, uncovered, for an additional 10 minutes.

Bring beef cubes and tomato base to the table in separate bowls. To serve, place some of the tomato mixture on a serving plate and top with some of the beef cubes. If desired, serve with rice cooked in beef bouillon and a green salad. Serves 6.

Tangy Beef Stew

3 tablespoons polyunsat-
  urated oil

2 medium onions,
  chopped

3 pounds top or bottom round or other lean beef (all visible fat removed), cut into 2-inch cubes
1 clove garlic, minced
Salt and freshly ground pepper to taste

¼ teaspoon celery salt
½ teaspoon thyme
½ cup beef bouillon
½ cup red wine
2 tablespoons lemon juice
Dash Tabasco sauce
¼ teaspoon anchovy paste

Heat oil in a heavy pot or Dutch oven. Add onion, beef cubes, and garlic and sauté until beef is lightly browned on all sides and onion is golden. Stir in salt, pepper, celery salt, thyme, beef bouillon, and wine. Bring to a boil, cover, and simmer over low heat 1½ hours or until meat is tender. Stir in lemon juice, Tabasco sauce, and anchovy paste. Simmer 5 minutes. Serves 6.

Tipsy Beef

1½ pounds flank steak (all visible fat removed)
1½ tablespoons lemon juice
½ tablespoon soy sauce
1 clove garlic, minced
1 tablespoon sesame seed oil
3 tablespoons polyunsaturated oil
3 thin slices fresh ginger or ½ teaspoon ground ginger

1 onion, sliced in thin rings
1 green pepper, seeded and sliced in julienne strips
¼ pound fresh mushrooms, sliced vertically into thirds
Salt and pepper to taste
1 tablespoon cornstarch
⅓ cup beer

Slice steak across the grain into ¼-inch thick slices, about 2½ inches long. Mix lemon juice, soy sauce, garlic, and sesame seed oil. Add beef slices and stir until they are coated evenly. Marinate in refrigerator at least 1 hour, stirring occasionally.

Heat oil in a wok or heavy skillet over medium heat. Add the beef slices (undrained—most of marinade should be absorbed) and stir-fry until meat is lightly browned, about 1 minute. Add ginger, onion, and green pepper. Stir-fry 2 minutes. Add mushrooms and continue to stir-fry 1 minute longer. Add salt and pepper to taste.

Mix cornstarch and beer, stirring until mixture is free of lumps. Add to the wok, bring mixture to a boil, and cook, stirring constantly, until the mixture thickens and turns opaque. Serve with rice. Serves 4.

Zippy Steak

1 2-pound steak, trimmed of all visible fat	1 tablespoon steak sauce
	2 teaspoons Worcestershire sauce
2 tablespoons tomato juice	½ teaspoon dry mustard
	2 cloves garlic, minced

Place steak on broiling pan and broil 6 minutes per side or until desired degree of doneness is reached. While steak is cooking, combine remaining ingredients in a small, heavy saucepan. Cook, stirring, for 2 minutes. Pour on broiled steak. Serves 4.

Apple Meat Loaf

1 pound lean ground round (or half beef, half veal)	⅓ cup quick-cooking oatmeal
	Salt and freshly ground pepper to taste
1 onion, chopped fine	
1 apple, peeled, cored, and diced fine	1 tablespoon prepared brown mustard

1½ tablespoons prepared
white horseradish
1 teaspoon curry powder

½ teaspoon garlic powder
¼ cup nonfat dry milk
dissolved in ⅓ cup
water

Mix ground round, onion, apple, oatmeal, salt, pepper, mustard, horseradish, curry powder, garlic powder, and milk. Shape into a loaf and transfer to an 8- or 9-inch loaf pan. Bake in preheated 350°F. oven for 1 hour or until desired degree of doneness is reached. Pour off any fat before serving. Serves 4.

Fruited Meat Loaf

1 pound lean ground
round (or half beef,
half veal)
¼ cup quick-cooking
oatmeal
1 pear, washed, cored,
and grated (do not peel)
1 onion, chopped fine

1 tablespoon lemon juice
½ teaspoon salt
¼ teaspoon pepper
½ teaspoon ground
ginger
Scant ½ teaspoon
allspice
¼ teaspoon dry mustard
2 tablespoons duck sauce

Mix ground round, oatmeal, grated pear, onion, lemon juice, salt, pepper, ginger, allspice, and mustard. Shape into a loaf and place in a loaf pan. Bake at 350°F. for 1 hour or until meat has just reached desired degree of doneness. Drain off any accumulated fat. Dribble the duck sauce over the loaf. Bake an additional 5 minutes. Serves 4.

Honey Burgers

1 pound lean ground
round
1 small onion, chopped
fine

¼ teaspoon dry mustard
⅛ teaspoon garlic powder
Salt and freshly ground
pepper to taste

1 tablespoon steak sauce   1 tablespoon honey

Combine ground round, onion, mustard, garlic powder, salt and pepper, steak sauce, and honey. Mix (use your hands) until all ingredients are well distributed. Shape into 4 patties. Broil 5 to 7 minutes per side or until desired degree of doneness is reached. Serves 4.

Lasagne

2 tablespoons polyunsaturated oil
1 pound lean ground beef
2 onions, chopped
1 clove garlic, minced
1 teaspoon basil
1 tablespoon minced parsley
½ teaspoon oregano
1 teaspoon salt
½ teaspoon pepper

1 28-ounce can tomatoes, chopped (do not drain)
1 6-ounce can tomato paste
2 tablespoons red wine
1 1-pound package lasagne noodles
1 1-pound container low-fat cottage cheese
2 tablespoons partially skimmed grated Parmesan cheese

Heat oil in a heavy skillet or Dutch oven. Stir in beef, onion, and garlic and sauté until beef loses its red color and onion is golden. Break up beef while sautéing. Add basil, parsley, oregano, salt, pepper, tomatoes, tomato paste, and wine. Bring to a boil, cover, and simmer over low heat for 30 minutes. While sauce is cooking, cook lasagne noodles according to package directions and drain.

Preheat oven to 325°F.

Grease a shallow 10- by 14-inch baking dish with diet or special margarine (page 21). Place one layer of noodles over the bottom. Spread one half of the cottage cheese over noodles. Top with one third of the sauce. Repeat to make a second layer. For the third layer, spread a layer of lasagne noodles and top with the remaining one third of the sauce. Sprinkle grated Parmesan cheese over all. Bake in a 325°F. oven for 25 minutes. Serves 4 to 6.

Mock Cutlets

4 slices white bread
1 pound lean ground round
2 egg whites
1 small onion, grated
1 clove garlic, minced

3 tablespoons green pepper, finely chopped
½ teaspoon paprika
2 tablespoons plus 1 teaspoon tomato juice
1 teaspoon basil
1½ cups corn flakes
2 tablespoons polyunsaturated oil

Moisten bread with water. Squeeze bread to remove as much of the water as possible. Tear bread into small pieces. In a large mixing bowl, combine bread pieces with meat. Add egg whites, grated onion, garlic, green pepper, paprika, tomato juice, and basil. Shape the meat into oval patties. Crush corn flakes by placing them between 2 pieces of waxed paper and rolling over them with a rolling pin. Cover patties with cornflakes on both sides. Make light crisscross (waffle) patterns on both sides of the patties. Heat oil in a large skillet. Sauté the patties in the oil until they are browned on both sides, about 5 minutes per side, or to desired degree of doneness. Serves 2 to 3.

Sauerkraut Meat Loaf

1½ pounds lean ground round
1 cup drained sauerkraut
1 tablespoon caraway seeds

½ apple, peeled, cored, and diced
¼ cup quick-cooking oatmeal
½ teaspoon dry mustard

¼ cup sauerkraut liquid
⅓ cup tomato juice

Salt and freshly ground
pepper to taste

Preheat oven to 350°F.

Mix beef, sauerkraut, caraway seeds, apple, oatmeal, dry mustard, sauerkraut liquid, tomato juice, and salt and pepper. Shape into a loaf and place in a loaf pan. Bake at 350°F. for 1 hour or until desired degree of doneness is reached. Pour off any fat before serving. Serves 6.

Sesame Burgers

1½ tablespoons polyun-
    saturated oil
1 onion, chopped
1 pound lean ground
    round
2 teaspoons sesame seeds

¼ teaspoon ground
    coriander
Salt and freshly ground
    pepper to taste
3 tablespoons beef stock
    or bouillon

Heat oil in a small skillet. Add onion and sauté until onion is lightly browned. Drain onions and add to ground round. Add sesame seeds, coriander, salt, pepper, and beef stock. Mix well and shape into 4 patties. Broil 5 to 7 minutes per side or until desired degree of doneness is reached. Serves 4.

Spaghetti and Meatballs

Meatballs:
2 pounds lean ground
    round
½ teaspoon oregano
    Salt and freshly ground
    pepper to taste
1 teaspoon polyunsatur-
    ated oil (optional)

Sauce:
1 6-ounce can tomato
    paste
1 6-ounce can water
6 ounces red wine
1 1-pound 1-ounce can
    Italian style plum
    tomatoes

½ green pepper, seeded
  and chopped
1 onion, minced
2 cloves garlic, minced

1 teaspoon basil
1 bay leaf
½ teaspoon oregano
1 teaspoon parsley

1 pound spaghetti

Shape meat into small meatballs. Sprinkle with oregano, salt, and freshly ground pepper. Brown meatballs in a very large skillet (use 1 teaspoon oil if meat is extremely lean to prevent sticking). Pour off any excess fat. Add spaghetti sauce ingredients to the browned meatballs. Mix and cook, uncovered, over low heat for 1 hour.

Cook spaghetti according to package directions and drain. Place the spaghetti in a large serving bowl. Pour the sauce over the spaghetti and mix, arranging the meatballs on top. Serve with red wine, and a tossed green salad with Italian dressing. Serves 4.

Aegean Lamb

2 to 2½ pounds boneless
  lamb cut from the leg
  or shoulder (all visible
  fat removed)
3 tablespoons polyun-
  saturated oil
4 small whole yellow
  onions, peeled
⅔ cup beef bouillon
1 teaspoon rosemary
1 clove garlic, minced

2 tablespoons lemon
  juice
  Salt and pepper to taste
1 eggplant (about 1¼
  pounds)
1 9-ounce package frozen
  French-style green
  beans
1 teaspoon lemon peel,
  grated fine
2 tablespoons minced
  parsley

Preheat oven to 350°F. Cut lamb into 2-inch cubes. Heat the oil in a Dutch oven or casserole dish that can be placed over direct heat. Add lamb and sauté until lightly browned on all sides. Stir in onions, beef bouillon, rosemary, garlic, lemon juice, salt, and pepper. Bring to a boil on top of the stove. Cover. Bake in a 350°F. oven for 1 hour.

Wash eggplant but do not peel. Cut off stem end and discard. Cut into 1-inch cubes. Add eggplant cubes, green beans, lemon peel, and parsley to the lamb. Cover and bake for 30 more minutes. Serves 4.

Capered Leg of Lamb

1 5- to 6-pound leg of lamb	2 tablespoons lemon juice
2 cloves garlic, slivered	2 tablespoons white wine
2½ teaspoons anchovy paste	¼ cup minced parsley
	½ teaspoon drained capers, minced

Preheat oven to 325°F. Trim all visible fat from the lamb. Make small gashes in the lamb with a knife and insert a garlic sliver in each gash. Place lamb on a rack in a shallow roasting pan and set aside.

Combine anchovy paste, lemon juice, and wine. Stir in parsley and capers. Mix well and spread evenly all over lamb. Roast at 325°F. 25 minutes per pound or until lamb has reached desired degree of doneness. Skim any fat from pan juices before serving. Serves 6 to 8.

Dilled Lamb

3 tablespoons polyunsaturated oil	2 medium onions, chopped
2 pounds cubed lamb cut from the leg or shoulder (all visible fat removed)	1 teaspoon dried dill weed
	1 teaspoon salt
	¼ teaspoon pepper

¾ cup beef bouillon
2 tablespoons lemon
 juice
1 cup celery tops

2 stalks celery, chopped
1 10-ounce package
 frozen mixed
 vegetables

Preheat oven to 350°F. Heat oil in a heavy pot or Dutch oven. Add lamb and onions and sauté until lamb is browned on all sides and onions are golden. Stir in dill weed, salt, pepper, bouillon, lemon juice, and celery tops. Bring to a boil on top of the stove. Cover. Bake in a 350°F. oven for 45 minutes. Add chopped celery and bake an additional 45 minutes or until lamb is tender. Discard celery tops. Skim any fat from gravy. Add frozen mixed vegetables and bake an additional 15 minutes. Serves 4.

Indonesian Lamb

3 tablespoons polyun-
 saturated oil
3 pounds cubed lamb cut
 from the leg or
 shoulder (all visible fat
 removed)
3 onions, chopped coarse
1 clove garlic, minced
2 teaspoons curry
 powder
1 teaspoon turmeric
1 teaspoon ground
 coriander

¼ teaspoon cumin seed,
 crushed
 Salt and freshly ground
 pepper to taste
½ cup beef bouillon
2 stalks celery, sliced
1 apple, peeled, cored,
 and diced
1 tablespoon lemon juice
½ cup skim milk
1 tablespoon flour
1 banana, peeled and
 diced

Heat oil in a Dutch oven or heavy pot. Add lamb, onions, and garlic and sauté until the lamb is browned on all sides and onion is transparent. Stir in the curry powder, turmeric, coriander, cumin seed, salt, and pepper. Add bouillon and mix well. Bring to a boil on top of the stove. Cover. Bake in a 350°F. oven for 45 minutes.

Add celery, apple, and lemon juice. Cover and bake an additional 45 minutes. Mix milk and flour together with a whisk until mixture is free of lumps. Stir diced banana and milk mixture into the lamb. Cover and bake 15 minutes. Serve with rice if desired. Serves 6.

Lamb in Red Wine

3 tablespoons polyun-
   saturated oil
2½ pounds boneless lamb
   from the leg or
   shoulder (all visible fat
   removed), cut into 1½-
   inch cubes
2 cloves garlic, minced
1 tablespoon soy sauce

⅔ cup red wine
1 teaspoon prepared
   brown mustard
¼ teaspoon marjoram
4 whole onions, peeled
3 carrots, peeled and
   sliced
1 tablespoon minced
   parsley

Heat oil in a heavy pot or Dutch oven. Add lamb and garlic and sauté until lamb cubes are browned on all sides. Stir in soy sauce, red wine, mustard, and marjoram. Bring to a boil, cover, and simmer over low heat for 1 hour. Stir in onions, carrots, and parsley. Cover and simmer 1 hour more or until vegetables are tender. Serves 4 to 6.

Leg of Lamb with Potatoes

1 5- to 6-pound leg of
   lamb (all visible fat
   removed)
1 clove garlic, slivered
   Salt and freshly ground
   pepper to taste
2 onions, chopped

2 pounds potatoes,
   peeled and sliced
   ¼ inch thick
2 tablespoons lemon
   juice
½ cup white wine
1 teaspoon dried dill
   weed

Preheat oven to 325°F. Make gashes all over lamb with a small knife. Insert a garlic sliver in each gash. Place on a rack in a shallow roasting pan and sprinkle with salt and pepper to taste. Put onions and potatoes over the bottom of the pan. Mix lemon juice, white wine, and dill weed. Pour over lamb. Roast at 325°F. for 25 minutes per pound or until desired degree of doneness is reached. Baste occasionally. Pour off any accumulated fat before serving. Serves 6 to 8.

Minted Lamb Chops

4 loin lamb chops	Salt and freshly ground pepper to taste
	2 teaspoons mint jelly

Preheat broiler. Trim all the visible fat from lamb chops and let stand at room temperature for 30 minutes. Salt and pepper the chops. Broil on a rack about 2 inches from the source of heat. Cook about 10 minutes per side for rare, 15 minutes for medium, and 20 minutes for well done. Just before they are done, spread ½ teaspoon mint jelly over each chop and let chops broil about one minute or until the jelly is completely melted. Serves 4.

Roast Leg of Lamb Deluxe

1 5-pound leg of lamb, well trimmed of visible fat	1 shallot, minced
	½ teaspoon thyme
1 clove garlic, sliced	½ teaspoon parsley
Juice of 1 lemon	Salt and freshly ground pepper to taste

Preheat oven to 300°F. Pat meat dry with paper towels. Make several incisions in the meat and insert a garlic slice into each incision. Place on a roasting rack in a shallow pan.

Pour lemon juice and minced shallot over the roast. Sprinkle with thyme and parsley. Season with salt and pepper. Leave meat at room temperature for an hour before roasting. Insert a meat thermometer. Roast uncovered for 15 to 18 minutes per pound for medium rare (145° to 150°F. on meat thermometer) or 18 to 20 minutes per pound for well done (160° to 165°F.). Serve with mint jelly. Serves 6.

Shish Kebab

2	pounds lean lamb shoulder (all visible fat removed), cut into 1½-inch cubes	¼	teaspoon salt Freshly ground pepper to taste
⅓	cup polyunsaturated oil Juice of 1 lemon	2	onions, cut into quarters (cut horizontally, then vertically)
2	tablespoons wine vinegar	1	green pepper, seeded and cut into 1-inch pieces
1	clove garlic, minced		
½	teaspoon thyme	12	cherry tomatoes
¼	teaspoon rosemary	12	mushroom caps

Place lamb cubes in a large glass mixing bowl. Combine oil, lemon juice, wine vinegar, garlic, thyme, rosemary, salt, and pepper. Pour over the meat and cover. Let meat marinate in refrigerator for 4 hours or more. Drain. Put one piece of meat on each of 6 skewers followed by an onion quarter, a green pepper slice, a cherry tomato, and a mushroom cap. Continue threading the remaining meat and vegetables in the same manner until all the meat and vegetables are used. Broil or cook on a charcoal grill for 6 to 8 minutes, turning the meat as it cooks, until it is browned on all sides. Serves 6.

Stuffed Pork Chops

8	pork chops	⅓	cup applesauce
1½	cups fine bread crumbs	⅛	teaspoon cinnamon

2 teaspoons fresh onion, minced

1 tablespoon poly-unsaturated oil

Salt and freshly ground pepper to taste

2 medium apples, each cut into 4 slices

½ teaspoon basil

Preheat oven to 400°F. Trim all visible fat from the pork chops. Cut a small pocket horizontally though the center of each chop. Mix together bread crumbs, applesauce, cinnamon, and minced onion. Set aside. Heat oil in a heavy skillet. Brown chops in the oil. When browned, place in a shallow baking pan. Fill each chop with the bread crumb mixture. Salt and pepper the chops. Top each chop with an apple slice and sprinkle each slice with basil. Cover and bake at 400°F. for 40 minutes. Serves 4.

Sweet and Sour Pork Chops

2 tablespoons sesame seed oil

4 loin pork chops, well trimmed of visible fat

3 tablespoons ketchup

3 tablespoons white vinegar

3 tablespoons sugar

¼ cup pineapple juice (from 1 8-ounce can pineapple chunks)

2 tablespoons cornstarch combined with ¼ cup cold water

1 onion, cut into bite-sized pieces

2 large tomatoes, cut into bite-sized pieces

1 green pepper, seeded and cut into bite-sized pieces

1 8-ounce can pineapple chunks, drained

Place 1 tablespoon sesame seed oil in a heavy skillet. Add the chops and brown well on both sides over brisk heat. Cover, reduce the heat, and cook the chops until well done, about 20 minutes.

Combine ketchup, vinegar, sugar, pineapple juice, and cornstarch mixture in a large saucepan. Over low heat bring sauce to a boil, stirring constantly. Remove from heat immediately. Heat the remaining tablespoon of sesame seed oil in a skillet or wok. Add onion, tomatoes, and green pepper all at once and stir fry for 1 minute. Add vegetables to the sauce. Pat pork chops dry with paper towels to remove excess fat. Place chops on a warm platter. Just before serving, add pineapple chunks to the sauce. (They should be just warmed — not cooked through.) Pour sauce over chops. Serves 4.

Baked Veal Chops

1½ pounds lean loin or shoulder veal chops (all visible fat removed)	⅓ cup skim milk Dash Tabasco sauce
1 teaspoon salt	½ cup crushed corn flakes or bread crumbs
¼ teaspoon pepper	1 teaspoon parsley flakes
	1 tablespoon lemon juice

Soak veal chops in a mixture of salt, pepper, milk, and Tabasco sauce. Dip in crushed corn flakes and refrigerate for 1 hour.

Preheat oven to 375°F. Grease a shallow baking dish with polyunsaturated oil, place chops in dish, and bake, uncovered, at 375°F. for 1 hour or until chops are tender. Sprinkle chops with parsley flakes and dribble on lemon juice during the last 5 minutes of baking. Serves 4.

Breaded Veal Cutlets

3 slices white bread	1 egg white, lightly beaten
1 teaspoon parsley, minced	3 tablespoons special margarine (page 21)
½ teaspoon oregano	½ cup partially skimmed mozarella cheese, shredded
½ teaspoon paprika	
1 clove garlic, minced	
4 loin veal chops	¼ cup chicken bouillon

Crumble the bread and put it in a blender container. Process until bread yields one cup of fine bread crumbs. Put crumbs in a shallow bowl. Add parsley, oregano, paprika, and minced garlic. Mix well. Set aside.

Put veal between 2 pieces of waxed paper and pound with a meat mallet or the edge of a saucer to tenderize. Dip each piece of veal in the egg white and then in the bread crumb mixture. Melt margarine in a large skillet. Add chops and brown on both sides, about 7 minutes to a side. Put mozarella cheese on top of each piece of veal. Add the chicken bouillon. Cover and cook for 10 minutes or until the cheese is melted and the veal is tender. Serves 4.

Country Fresh Veal

1½ pounds veal scallops
Salt and freshly ground
  pepper to taste
3 tablespoons special
  margarine (page 21)
½ cup dry white wine

2 tomatoes, cut into small
  pieces
¼ pound mushrooms,
  sliced
1 shallot, minced
1 teaspoon parsley flakes
¼ teaspoon thyme

Place veal between 2 pieces of waxed paper. Pound veal with a meat hammer or the edge of a heavy saucer until it is very thin. Cut into 2-inch pieces and season with salt and pepper. In a large, heavy skillet, sauté the veal in 2 tablespoons margarine until it is lightly browned, about 5 minutes. Add wine and tomatoes to the skillet and deglaze by forcing scrapings on the bottom and sides of the pan into the sauce. Bring wine to a boil and boil liquid until slightly reduced. In a small skillet, sauté mushrooms and shallot in 1 tablespoon margarine until lightly browned. Add mushrooms and shallots to the wine sauce. Place veal on a warm platter and pour the wine mixture over all. Sprinkle with parsley flakes and thyme. Serves 4.

Piquant Veal Birds

1 pound veal scallops
2 tablespoons poly-
  unsaturated oil
1 onion, chopped
1 carrot, peeled and
  grated
½ cup grated cucumber
¼ cup pine nuts
½ teaspoon salt
¼ teaspoon pepper

¼ teaspoon dried dill
  weed
3 tablespoons poly-
  unsaturated oil
¼ cup chicken bouillon
¼ cup white wine
¼ cup evaporated skim
  milk
1 tablespoon flour
1½ teaspoon lemon juice
1 tablespoon minced
  parsley

Pound veal with a meat mallet or the edge of a heavy saucer until thin. Heat 2 tablespoons oil in a heavy skillet large enough to hold the veal. Add onions and sauté until translucent. Turn into a bowl and add the carrot, cucumber, pine nuts, salt, pepper, and dill weed. Mix well. Place a portion of the mixture on each veal scallop. Roll up and secure with string or toothpicks.

Heat the 3 tablespoons oil in the skillet. Add the veal rolls and sauté until veal is lightly browned on all sides. Set the rolls aside. Add the stock and wine to the skillet and cook over low heat 1 minute, deglazing the pan by scraping browned particles from the bottom and sides. Return veal rolls to the skillet, cover, and simmer 30 minutes, turning occasionally. Mix the milk and flour with a whisk until smooth. Stir the milk mixture, lemon juice, and parsley into the sauce. Cook 5 minutes or until heated through. Serves 3 to 4.

Romano Veal

1½ pounds veal scallops

¼ cup flour

Salt and freshly ground pepper to taste
2 tablespoons special margarine (page 21)
¼ cup dry white wine

1 beef bouillon cube dissolved in ¼ cup boiling water
8 cherry tomatoes, halved
½ teaspoon oregano

Place veal between 2 pieces of waxed paper. Pound the veal with a meat hammer or the edge of a heavy saucer until it is very thin. Put flour on a flat plate and season it with salt and pepper. Lightly flour each piece of veal. In a large skillet, melt the margarine and sauté the veal until it is browned on both sides. Add wine, beef bouillon, cherry tomatoes, and oregano. Force any scrapings on the bottom of the pan into the sauce. Cook, uncovered, 2 more minutes, until the tomatoes are just soft. Remove veal to a serving platter. Pour sauce over veal. Serves 4.

Veal Capri

1½ pounds veal scallops, cut into bite-sized pieces
4 tablespoons special margarine (page 21)
1 onion, chopped
⅓ cup chicken bouillon

1 teaspoon safflower oil
1 10-ounce package frozen chopped broccoli, defrosted
9 cherry tomatoes, halved
¼ teaspoon tarragon

Put veal between 2 pieces of waxed paper and pound with a mallet or the edge of a saucer until thin. Melt 3 tablespoons margarine in a large skillet. Sauté the onion until transparent. Add the veal and brown on both sides. Add chicken bouillon and bring to a boil. Boil for 3 minutes or until slightly reduced. In a medium-sized, heavy skillet, heat the remaining 1 tablespoon margarine with 1 teaspoon safflower oil until margarine melts. Sauté broccoli for 3 minutes, stirring constantly. Add the broccoli and tomatoes to the veal. Sprinkle with tarragon.

Cook, uncovered, stirring constantly, until all the liquid is absorbed, 5 to 10 minutes. Serves 4.

Veal Piccata

1½ pounds veal scallops	2 tablespoons lemon
Salt and freshly ground	juice
pepper to taste	1 lemon, sliced very thin
4 tablespoons special	½ teaspoon thyme
margarine (page 21)	

Place the veal between 2 pieces of waxed paper and pound very thin with a meat hammer or the edge of a heavy saucer. Cut into 2-inch pieces and season with salt and pepper. In a large skillet, sauté the veal in 2 tablespoons margarine until lightly browned on both sides (about 5 minutes). Remove the veal and place on a serving platter. Put the platter in a low oven to keep warm. Add the remaining 2 tablespoons margarine and lemon juice to the skillet. Deglaze the pan by forcing any scrapings on the bottom and sides of the pan into the sauce. Remove veal platter from the oven. When margarine has melted, pour sauce over the veal and garnish lemon slices and thyme. Serves 4.

Veal Roll-ups

1 medium potato, peeled	¼ teaspoon thyme
2 tablespoons poly-	Dash sage
unsaturated oil	1 pound veal scallops
1 onion, chopped	3 tablespoons (addi-
1½ teaspoons anchovy	tional) polyunsaturated
paste	oil
½ teaspoon salt	½ cup chicken bouillon
¼ teaspoon pepper	1 tablespoon lemon juice

1 bay leaf	2 teaspoons minced parsley

Put potato in water to cover. Boil until tender, about 10 minutes. Drain. When potato is cool enough to handle, place in a small bowl and chop fine. Set aside.

Heat the 2 tablespoons oil in a heavy skillet large enough to hold the veal roll-ups. Add the chopped onion and sauté until onion is golden. Add onion, anchovy paste, salt, pepper, thyme, and sage to the potato. Mix well and set aside.

Lay veal out on a flat surface and pound thin with a meat mallet or the edge of a heavy saucer. Place a portion of the potato mixture on each scallop and roll up. Secure roll-ups with string or toothpicks. Heat the 3 tablespoons oil in the skillet in which the onions have been sautéed. Sauté the roll-ups until they are lightly browned on all sides. Set veal rolls aside and add the chicken bouillon to the pan. Deglaze by cooking 1 minute over medium heat and scraping the bottom and sides of the pan to loosen any browned particles. Stir in lemon juice and bay leaf. Return veal rolls to pan. Cover and simmer 20 to 25 minutes over low heat or until veal is tender. Stir in parsley and simmer 1 minute longer.

Place veal roll-ups on a warm serving dish and measure sauce in pan. If not reduced to ⅓ cup, boil, uncovered, over high heat until reduced. Pour over roll-ups and serve. Serves 3 to 4.

Veal with Peppers

1½ pounds veal scallops	Salt and freshly ground pepper to taste
3 tablespoons special margarine (page 21)	1 chicken bouillon cube dissolved in ¼ cup boiling water
1 large onion, sliced	¼ teaspoon oregano
1 large green pepper, seeded and sliced	

Place veal between two pieces of waxed paper and pound very thin. Melt 2 tablespoons margarine in a large skillet.

Add the onion and green pepper. Season with salt and freshly ground pepper. Sauté until the onion is transparent. Remove onion and green pepper to a serving platter. Add the remaining tablespoon of margarine. When it has melted, brown the veal on both sides. Add chicken bouillon, forcing any scrapings on the bottom of the pan into the liquid. Add cooked onion and pepper. Cook, uncovered, allowing the bouillon to boil until almost all the liquid is absorbed (5 to 10 minutes). Serves 4.

Veal with Spaghetti

2 pounds boneless veal shoulder, trimmed of all visible fat and cut in ½-inch cubes
¼ cup flour
½ teaspoon salt
¼ teaspoon pepper
¼ cup polyunsaturated oil
2 cloves garlic, minced
2 onions, chopped
1 28-ounce can tomatoes, chopped (do not drain)
1 6-ounce can tomato paste
½ cup white wine
½ teaspoon anchovy paste
1 teaspoon basil
½ teaspoon oregano
¼ teaspoon thyme
¼ teaspoon pepper
1 green pepper, seeded and cut into strips
¼ pound mushrooms, sliced in vertical thirds
1 tablespoon minced parsley
2 pounds spaghetti
2 tablespoons special margarine (page 21)
1 tablespoon minced parsley

Dredge veal in a mixture of the flour, salt, and pepper. Heat oil in a large skillet or Dutch oven. Add veal cubes, garlic, and onions. Sauté until veal is lightly browned and the onion is wilted. Add tomatoes and liquid, tomato paste, wine, anchovy paste, basil, oregano, thyme, and pepper. Mix well. Bring to a boil, cover, and simmer over low heat for 20 minutes. Uncover and simmer 15 minutes or until veal is tender and sauce has thickened. Add green pepper, mushrooms, and parsley. Simmer, covered, for 10 minutes.

While sauce is cooking, cook spaghetti according to package directions. Drain well in colander and toss with the margarine and parsley. Top spaghetti with veal sauce. Serves 8.

7
Poultry

Traditional Thanksgiving and Christmas dinners don't have to suffer because of a low cholesterol eating plan. Chicken and turkey are low in saturated fat and cholesterol, and they make excellent choices for festive occasions. However, do stay away from duck and goose, which are much too fatty. In using the following poultry recipes, let your imagination be your guide. Chicken, turkey, Cornish hen, and capon adapt well to a wide variety of sauces and stuffings.

Do Not Use
  Duck
  Goose
  Poultry fat
  Poultry giblets (including giblets from recommended poultry)

Do Use
  Capon
  Chicken
  Chicken bouillon and canned chicken broth
  Cornish hen
  Squab
  Turkey

Helpful Hints
Remove poultry skin after cooking but before serving. This is very important since the skin is high in saturated fat.

The light meat of poultry is leaner than the dark meat. However, even the dark meat is lower in saturated fat than most trimmed beef, pork, or lamb.

When you roast poultry, use the smallest possible roasting pan so that the drippings will not spread too thin and scorch the pan.

Poultry stuffing can be made in advance. However, the stuffing should be stored in a separate dish until you are ready to cook the poultry. The bird should not be stuffed until immediately prior to roasting because organisms can grow in the climate created in the prestuffed bird that can cause serious illness. Leftover poultry and stuffing should be stored separately.

Baked Chicken and Rice Deluxe

3 tablespoons poly-
  unsaturated oil
1 onion, chopped
1 stalk celery, chopped
3½ cups cooked rice
1 apple, peeled, cored,
  and diced
2 tablespoons slivered
  almonds
¼ teaspoon poultry
  seasoning

Salt and freshly ground
  pepper to taste
1 3½-pound frying
  chicken (all visible fat
  removed), cut up into
  serving-sized pieces
1 tablespoon grated
  lemon rind
¼ cup fresh lemon juice
⅔ cup orange juice
½ cup chicken bouillon

¼ cup white wine

¼ teaspoon ginger

¼ cup brown sugar

Preheat oven to 350°F. Heat oil in a small skillet. Add onion and celery and sauté until onion is translucent. Stir into cooked rice. Add apple, almonds, poultry seasoning, salt, and pepper to taste. Mix well. Spread mixture over the bottom of a shallow baking dish. Rub chicken pieces with salt and pepper and arrange on top of rice.

Mix lemon rind, lemon juice, orange juice, bouillon, wine, brown sugar, and ginger in a small saucepan. Bring to a boil and simmer, uncovered, for 5 minutes. Pour over chicken pieces in pan. Bake at 350°F. for 1 hour or until all is tender. Serves 4.

Burgundy Roast Chicken

Stuffing:

2 tablespoons special margarine (page 21)

1 onion, chopped fine

1½ cup bread crumbs

1 tablespoon fresh parsley, chopped

¼ cup chicken bouillon

1 3½-pound chicken (all visible fat removed)

Sauce:

¼ cup special margarine

¾ cup Burgundy wine

Preheat oven to 350°F. Melt the margarine in a heavy skillet. Add the onions and sauté until the onions are transparent. Add bread crumbs and continue sautéing until they are lightly browned. Add the parsley and chicken bouillon and cook, stirring constantly, until all the liquid is absorbed (2 to 3 minutes). Stuff the chicken lightly with the mixture and truss. Place chicken, breast side up, on a roasting rack.

Melt ¼ cup special margarine in a small saucepan. Add wine. Brush the stuffed chicken liberally with the wine mixture and baste frequently during roasting. Roast at 350°F. for 1¼ hours or until chicken is golden brown and tender. Serves 4.

Chicken Afrique

3 tablespoons poly-unsaturated oil
1 3-pound frying chicken, all visible fat removed and cut up into serving-sized pieces
2 onions, chopped
1 stalk celery, chopped
½ teaspoon salt
¼ teaspoon pepper
½ teaspoon cinnamon
Pinch saffron
1 teaspoon ground coriander
¼ teaspoon turmeric
1 tablespoon honey
1 tablespoon lemon juice
½ cup chablis
1 apple, peeled, cored, and diced
3 tablespoons slivered almonds
¼ cup fresh parsley, minced
1 teaspoon grated lemon peel

Preheat oven to 350°F. Heat the oil in a heavy pot or Dutch oven. Sauté chicken, onion, and celery until chicken is golden and onion is translucent. Add salt, pepper, cinnamon, saffron, coriander, turmeric, lemon juice, honey, chablis, apple, and almonds to the chicken pieces. Stir well. Bring to a boil on top of the stove. Cover and bake in a 350°F. oven for 50 minutes. Stir in parsley and lemon peel and bake an additional 5 minutes or until all is tender. Serve over rice if desired. Serves 4.

Chicken in Cherry Sauce

¼ cup flour
1 teaspoon salt
¼ teaspoon pepper
¼ teaspoon ground allspice
1 3½-pound fryer (all visible fat removed) cut up into serving-sized pieces
3 tablespoons poly-unsaturated oil

1 onion, chopped fine
½ teaspoon celery seed
⅓ cup orange juice
1 1-pound can dark
   sweet cherries, pitted

2 tablespoons cornstarch
2 tablespoons lemon
   juice
1 teaspoon lemon peel,
   grated fine
½ teaspoon dry mustard

Mix flour, salt, pepper, and allspice in a paper bag. Add chicken pieces, a few at a time, and shake well until they are lightly but completely coated with flour mixture.

Heat oil in a Dutch oven. Add chicken pieces and chopped onion and sauté until chicken is lightly browned on all sides and onion is golden. Stir in celery seed and orange juice. Bring to a boil, cover, and simmer over low heat for 35 minutes. Set chicken aside and keep warm. Skim fat from the pan juices. (Dish may be cooked ahead to this point, and gravy may be frozen or refrigerated to harden fat.)

Drain cherries, reserving syrup. Mix 1 cup syrup with the cornstarch until mixture is free of lumps. Add to the pan gravy and cook, uncovered, over medium heat until mixture is thickened and clear, about 2 minutes. Stir in lemon juice, grated lemon peel, and dry mustard. Return chicken pieces to the Dutch oven and gently stir in the cherries. Cook, covered, over low heat until all is heated through. Serves 4.

Chicken in Cream Sauce

1 teaspoon salt
¼ teaspoon pepper
3 tablespoons flour
1 3-pound frying chicken
   (all visible fat removed),
   cut up into serving-
   sized pieces

3 tablespoons poly-
   unsaturated oil
1 tablespoon chopped
   shallots
¼ cup dry white wine
½ teaspoon thyme

2 tablespoons slivered almonds	1 tablespoon minced parsley
¼ cup mushrooms, cut into thirds vertically	¼ cup evaporated skim milk
	1 tablespoon flour

Mix salt, pepper, and flour. Dredge chicken pieces in the mixture. Heat the oil in a heavy pot or Dutch oven and sauté chicken pieces until they are lightly browned on all sides. Set aside.

Add shallots to the Dutch oven and sauté until they are browned. Add wine. Cook over medium high heat for 1 minute, deglazing pan by scraping the browned particles from the bottom and sides of the pan. Return chicken pieces to the Dutch oven and add thyme and almonds. Bring to a boil, cover, and simmer over low heat for 35 minutes. Add mushrooms and parsley. Mix the milk and flour. Stir with a whisk until mixture is free of lumps. Add milk-flour mixture to the chicken. Stir well. Simmer, covered, 5 minutes or until all is heated through and tender. Serve over rice if desired. Serves 4.

Chicken Lexington

3 tablespoons special margarine (page 21)	5 pieces 3- or 4-day old white bread (crusts removed), torn into coarse crumbs
1 3-pound chicken, quartered Salt and freshly ground pepper to taste	2 teaspoons parsley, minced
1 onion, finely chopped	½ teaspoon thyme
	½ teaspoon basil
	½ cup chicken broth
	⅓ cup V-8 juice or tomato juice

Preheat oven to 350°F. Melt 2 tablespoons margarine in a large skillet. Season chicken with salt and pepper and brown on both sides. Remove from skillet. Add 1 tablespoon margarine to skillet. Melt margarine and then sauté the onion until transparent. Place bread crumbs in a large bowl. Add sautéed onions, parsley, thyme, and basil to crumbs. Mix well. Place bread crumbs in the bottom of a greased baking dish. Place chicken on top. Combine chicken broth and tomato juice and pour over all. Bake covered at 350°F. for 30 minutes. Uncover and bake for 30 additional minutes. Serves 4.

Chicken Mayonnaise

½ cup mayonnaise (page 56)
1 tablespoon lemon juice
1 teaspoon Worcestershire sauce
½ teaspoon paprika
¼ teaspoon garlic powder
1 teaspoon salt
Pepper to taste
1 tablespoon minced parsley
1 tablespoon grated onion
1 3-pound frying chicken (all visible fat and skin removed), cut up into serving-sized pieces
1 cup soft bread crumbs
3 tablespoons special margarine, melted (page 21)

Preheat oven to 375°F. Mix mayonnaise, lemon juice, Worcestershire sauce, paprika, garlic powder, salt, pepper, parsley, and onion in a small bowl. Stir well. With special margarine grease a shallow baking dish large enough to hold chicken pieces in a single layer.

Dip chicken pieces into the mayonnaise mixture until coated and then into the bread crumbs. Place each finished piece in the prepared baking dish. When all the chicken has been prepared, place the dish in the oven and bake 1 hour or until chicken is browned and tender. Baste with melted margarine after 30 minutes. Serves 4.

Chicken Teriyaki

3 tablespoons poly-
unsaturated oil

1 3-pound frying chicken
(all visible fat removed),
cut up into serving-
sized pieces

1 medium onion, chopped

1 11-ounce can Mandarin
orange segments

¼ cup Teriyaki sauce

1 teaspoon prepared
brown mustard

1½ teaspoon white vinegar

2 tablespoons sesame
seed oil

1 clove garlic, minced

2 stalks celery, cut in
2-inch lengths and
quartered vertically

1 green pepper, seeded
and cut in julienne
strips

1 tablespoon cornstarch

Preheat oven to 350°F. Heat oil in a flameproof casserole or
Dutch oven. Sauté chicken pieces and chopped onion until
chicken is golden brown on all sides and onion is translucent.
Set aside.

Drain syrup from oranges and pour syrup into the casserole.
Stir in the Teriyaki sauce, mustard, vinegar, sesame seed
oil, and garlic. Bring to a boil and add chicken, onion, and
celery. Cover and transfer to oven. Bake at 350°F. for 50
minutes. Add green pepper, cornstarch, and orange segments.
Stir well and cook 5 minutes or until all is tender. Serve over
rice if desired. Serves 4.

Elegant Stuffed Chicken

2 whole chicken breasts,
skinned and boned, or
1½ pounds skinless
and boneless chicken
cutlets

2 tablespoons poly-
unsaturated oil

3 shallots, minced

¼ pound mushrooms,
chopped

¼ cup minced parsley

1½ tablespoons lemon
juice

½ teaspoon poultry
seasoning

2 tablespoons additional
polyunsaturated oil
⅔ cup liquid reserved
from canned tomatoes
½ cup drained canned
tomatoes, chopped
¼ teaspoon basil

Salt and freshly ground
pepper to taste
¼ cup evaporated skim
milk
1 tablespoon flour
1 tablespoon dehydrated
chives

Cut each chicken breast in half vertically, ending up with 4 pieces of raw chicken. Pound pieces with a meat mallet or the edge of a heavy saucer and set aside.

Heat the oil in a heavy skillet that has a cover. Sauté the shallots and mushrooms for 5 minutes. Stir in parsley, 1 table-spoon of the lemon juice, and poultry seasoning. Mix well. Put ¼ of the mixture on each chicken piece and roll up jelly-roll fashion. Tie with string or secure with toothpicks.

Heat the additional 2 tablespoons oil in the skillet. Add chicken rolls and sauté until lightly browned on all sides. Add the remaining lemon juice, tomato liquid, tomatoes, basil, salt, and pepper to taste. Bring to a boil and cover. Simmer over low heat for 30 minutes, turning rolls occasionally. Mix milk and flour with a whisk until smooth. Add, with the chives, to the skillet. Stir and simmer 5 minutes or until heated through. Serves 3 to 4.

Herbed Lemon Chicken

1 3½-pound chicken,
quartered
⅓ cup corn oil
¼ cup lemon juice

½ teaspoon thyme
1 teaspoon parsley flakes
¼ teaspoon tarragon
Salt and freshly ground
pepper to taste

Place chicken in a glass bowl. Mix all other ingredients together. Brush on chicken and let marinate for several hours or overnight. Place chicken pieces on a roasting rack in a shallow pan and bake at 325°F. for 1 hour. Serves 4.

Lime Baked Chicken

1 3-pound chicken, quartered	¼ cup sesame seed oil
Salt and freshly ground pepper to taste	Juice of 2 limes
	2 scallions, chopped
	½ teaspoon paprika
	½ teaspoon thyme

Season chicken with salt and pepper. Combine remaining ingredients and marinate chicken in the mixture in the refrigerator for 3 hours or more. Brush the mixture on the chicken. Bake on a roasting rack in a shallow pan at 350°F. for 1 hour, turning and basting occasionally. Serves 4.

Mystery Chicken

1 to 1¼ pounds chicken cutlets (2 whole chicken breasts, skinned and boned)	2 thin slices ginger root
	1 scallion, quartered horizontally
2 tablespoons sesame seed oil	1 2-inch piece peeled cucumber, cut into eighths lengthwise
2 tablespoons soy sauce	3 tablespoons poly-unsaturated oil
1 tablespoon sherry or white wine	¼ cup chicken bouillon
½ teaspoon dry mustard	½ cup water chestnuts, drained and sliced thin
1 clove garlic, minced	

Pound chicken with a meat mallet or the edge of a heavy saucer. Cut each breast in half vertically so that there are 4 pieces.

Mix sesame seed oil, soy sauce, sherry, dry mustard, garlic, and ginger. Marinate chicken pieces in the mixture for 2 hours or longer in the refrigerator.

Drain chicken pieces, reserving marinade. Place 2 pieces of cucumber and a piece of scallion at one end of each chicken piece. Roll up lengthwise and secure with string or toothpicks. Heat oil in a skillet and sauté chicken rolls until lightly browned on all sides. Add marinade, bouillon, and water chestnuts to the skillet. Bring to a boil. Cover and simmer 25 minutes or until chicken is tender. Serve over rice if desired. Serves 3 to 4.

Pineapple Chicken

¼ teaspoon allspice
1 teaspoon salt
¼ teaspoon pepper
½ teaspoon paprika
1 3½-pound whole fryer
  or roaster, all visible
  fat removed

1 8¼-ounce can sliced
  pineapple
1 tablespoon soy sauce
¼ teaspoon dry mustard
2 onions, sliced
1 green pepper, seeded
  and sliced

Mix allspice, salt, pepper, and paprika. Rub spices on chicken, inside and out. Drain pineapple, reserving the juice. Set pineapple aside and mix the juice with the soy sauce and dry mustard. Place chicken on a rack in a shallow roasting pan. Place onions over the bottom of the roasting pan. Pour the pineapple juice mixture over the chicken, and set in a 350°F. oven. Roast for 1¼ hours or until chicken is browned and tender, basting occasionally with pineapple liquid in bottom of pan. Put green pepper strips and sliced pineapple in bottom of roasting pan during the last 15 minutes of cooking. Serves 4.

Shanghai Chicken

8 dried Chinese
  mushrooms*

3 tablespoons poly-
  unsaturated oil

---

* Dried Chinese mushrooms and star anise are available at Chinese and Japanese food markets and at some gourmet stores. If they are unavailable, use regular American mushrooms and leave out the anise.

1 3-pound frying chicken
(all visible fat removed),
cut into serving-sized
pieces
1 tablespoon honey
1 tablespoon soy sauce
1 tablespoon sesame
seed oil

1 teaspoon white vinegar
½ cup chicken bouillon
1 star anise
½ cup water chestnuts,
drained and sliced
¼ cup minced scallions
(use the green and
white)

Soak mushrooms in water to cover. Set aside.

Heat oil in a Dutch oven or heavy pot. Add chicken pieces and sauté until lightly browned on all sides. Add honey, soy sauce, sesame seed oil, vinegar, chicken bouillon, and star anise and stir until well mixed. Bring to a boil, cover, and simmer over low heat for 25 minutes.

Drain the mushrooms (reserving liquid for soup stock or rice). Cut in ¼-inch slices and add to chicken. Add water chestnuts and simmer an additional 10 minutes. Stir in the scallions and simmer 2 more minutes or until all is tender. Serve over rice (cooked with mushroom liquid from the drained mushrooms instead of water) if desired. Serves 4.

"Souper" Chicken

3 tablespoons special
margarine (page 21)
1 3-pound chicken (all
visible fat removed),
cut up into serving-
sized pieces
1 onion, chopped
¼ teaspoon celery salt
½ teaspoon thyme

Salt and freshly ground
pepper to taste
¼ teaspoon poultry
seasoning
1 10¾-ounce can
vegetarian
vegetable soup
½ cup water
½ cup raw rice

Preheat oven to 325°F. Melt margarine in a Dutch oven or flameproof casserole dish. Add chicken pieces and onion and sauté until chicken is golden brown and onion is translucent. Stir in celery salt, thyme, salt, pepper, and poultry seasoning. Cover and place in oven. Bake at 325°F. for 40 minutes.

Add the soup as it comes from the can, water, and rice. Stir well and cover again. Bake for 35 minutes or until chicken and rice are tender. Serves 4.

Sweet and Sour Chicken Casserole

3 tablespoons poly-
unsaturated oil

1 3-pound fryer (all visible fat removed), cut up into serving-sized pieces

1 cup chopped onion

1 clove garlic, minced

½ teaspoon ground ginger

½ teaspoon allspice
Dash Tabasco sauce

Salt and freshly ground pepper to taste

3 tablespoons tomato paste

½ cup chicken bouillon

1 9-ounce package frozen French-style green beans

1 10-ounce package frozen cauliflower

1 tablespoon brown sugar

3 tablespoons lemon juice

Heat oil in a heavy pot or Dutch oven. Add chicken pieces, onion, and garlic and sauté until chicken is golden brown on all sides and onion is translucent. Add ginger, allspice, Tabasco sauce, salt, and pepper. Stir well. Add tomato paste and chicken bouillon. Stir until well blended. Bring to a boil, cover, and simmer over low heat for 35 minutes. Add the frozen beans just as they come from the box and simmer 10 minutes, stirring occasionally.

Just before serving, cook cauliflower in a saucepan according to package directions. Drain and add to the chicken. Add brown sugar and lemon juice. Simmer 1 minute or until all is well blended and heated through. Serves 4.

Tarragon Roast Chicken

1 3- to 4-pound roaster or whole fryer (all visible fat removed)
½ teaspoon salt
¼ teaspoon pepper
1 tablespoon special margarine
1 teaspoon lemon juice
1 teaspoon tarragon
1 teaspoon minced parsley
4 carrots, peeled and sliced
2 stalks celery, sliced
4 small whole yellow onions
1 apple, peeled, cored, and diced
2 tablespoons special margarine (page 21)

Preheat oven to 350°F. Place chicken on a rack in a shallow roasting pan, breast side up. Sprinkle cavity with salt and pepper. Add margarine, lemon juice, tarragon, and parsley to the cavity.

Mix carrots, celery, onions, and apple together. Fill cavity loosely with some of the mixture and place the rest around the chicken. Dot chicken with the 2 tablespoons margarine. Roast uncovered at 350°F. for 1¼ hours or until chicken is evenly browned and tender. Baste occasionally. Serves 4.

Note: This dish can be made in an earthenware roaster if desired. Proceed as above, placing chicken in the roaster. Cover and bake at 475°F. for 90 minutes.

Cornish Hen in Red Wine Sauce

2 Cornish hens, about 1½ pounds each, defrosted and cleaned (all visible fat removed)
Salt and freshly ground pepper to taste
3 tablespoons special margarine (page 21)
2 onions, chopped
2 cups cooked rice or bread cubes
¼ cup raisins or currants, plumped
1 apple, peeled, cored, and diced
¼ cup pine nuts or blanched, slivered almonds

1 tablespoon minced
  parsley
1 tablespoon minced
  seeded pimiento

¼ teaspoon thyme
½ cup chicken bouillon
½ cup red wine

Place the Cornish hens on a rack in a shallow roasting pan and sprinkle inside and out with salt and pepper. Set aside.
  Preheat oven to 450°F.
  Melt margarine in a small skillet. Add onions and sauté until onion is translucent. Turn into a small bowl and add rice, raisins, apple, nuts, parsley, pimiento, and thyme. Mix gently. Add ¼ cup of the chicken bouillon and stir until all is well mixed. Stuff half the mixture into the cavity of each hen. Place in oven and roast at 450°F. for 20 minutes.
  Mix the remaining ¼ cup bouillon with the wine and pour over hens. Turn oven down to 350°F. and roast for an additional 40 minutes or until hens are browned and tender, basting occasionally. Serves 4.

Oven-Barbecued Cornish Hens

2 Cornish hens, about
  1½ pounds each (all
  visible fat removed)
  Salt and freshly ground
  pepper to taste
2 teaspoons minced
  parsley
1 lemon, halved

2 tablespoons ketchup
½ teaspoon dry mustard
¼ teaspoon garlic powder
  Dash Tabasco sauce
2 teaspoons steak sauce
1 teaspoon Worcester-
  shire sauce
2 onions, sliced

Preheat oven to 325°F. Sprinkle the hens inside and out with salt and pepper. Sprinkle 1 teaspoon minced parsley in the cavity of each hen. Rub each hen with lemon and place hens on a rack in a shallow roasting pan. Set aside.
  Squeeze remaining lemon juice into a small bowl. Add ketchup, dry mustard, garlic powder, Tabasco sauce, steak sauce, and Worcestershire sauce. Stir well and rub over the

hens. Place sliced onions over the bottom of the pan. Roast at 325°F. for 1½ hours or until hens are evenly browned and tender. Serves 4.

Rock Cornish Hens à l'Orange

2 Rock Cornish hens, 1½ to 2 pounds each (all visible fat removed)
¾ teaspoon salt
¼ teaspoon pepper
¼ teaspoon garlic powder
¼ teaspoon paprika
2 tablespoons poly-unsaturated oil
1 medium onion, chopped
1 stalk celery, chopped
3 cups cooked rice
½ apple, peeled, cored, and diced
½ teaspoon sage
½ teaspoon poultry seasoning
½ teaspoon salt
¼ teaspoon pepper
½ cup chicken bouillon
½ cup orange juice

Preheat oven to 325°F. Clean and defrost hens. Mix salt, pepper, and garlic powder and rub the hens inside and out with seasoning mixture. Rub paprika on the outside of both hens. Place on a rack in a shallow roasting pan and set aside.

Heat oil in a small skillet. Sauté onion and celery until onion is golden. Turn into a bowl and add the rice, apple, sage, poultry seasoning, salt, and pepper. Stir in the chicken bouillon and mix well. Stuff the cavity of each hen with the mixture and spread any additional stuffing over the bottom of the roasting pan.

Roast at 325°F. for 1½ hours or until tender. During the last half hour of roasting, pour off any accumulated fat and pour orange juice over the hens. Serves 4.

Roast Turkey Deluxe

1 10- to 12-pound turkey
3 tablespoons poly-unsaturated oil
2 stalks celery, chopped
2 onions, chopped
1½ teaspoons poultry seasoning

1½ teaspoons salt
½ teaspoon pepper
2 tablespoons chopped parsley
1 apple, peeled, cored, and diced

¼ cup chopped walnuts
2 small loaves French bread, cubed
¾ cup chicken bouillon
¾ teaspoon paprika
⅓ cup special margarine, melted (page 21)

Preheat oven to 325°F. Clean turkey and pat dry. Set aside.

Heat oil in a skillet. Add celery and onion and sauté until onion is translucent. Turn into a bowl. Stir in poultry seasoning, salt, pepper, parsley, apple, walnuts, and bread cubes. Stir in chicken bouillon. Stuff mixture into the cavity of the turkey. Rub paprika over turkey and place on a rack in a roasting pan. Brush with melted margarine and cover with a clean cloth or brown paper bag torn in half.

Roast turkey at 325°F. for 3½ hours or until joints move easily and turkey is brown. Baste frequently with skimmed pan drippings. Remove cloth during the last 30 minutes of roasting. Serves 12.

8

Fish

Since many types of fish contain only moderate amounts of cholesterol and all fish is low in saturated fat, fish can be served as often as desired. Fish is unusual, easy to prepare, delicious, and a marvelous way to introduce your friends to the wonders of low cholesterol cooking.

Do Not Use
Fish roe (including caviar)
Lobster
Oysters

Do Use
All fish (Even the so-called "fat fish" is lean in comparison to most red meat and is therefore acceptable.)

Shrimp and crab (If other food on day eaten is limited to 50 milligrams of cholesterol.)

Helpful Hints

When buying whole fish, allow 1 pound per person. When buying fish steaks or fillets, allow ⅓ to ½ pound per person.

If possible, serve fresh fish. All fish loses some flavor when frozen. Fish will keep up to three days in the refrigerator, but serve as soon as possible after buying for maximum flavor.

The most important hint for cooking fish is: *don't overcook.* Fish becomes dry, tough, and tasteless when overcooked. Fish is done when it separates from the bone and can be flaked with a fork.

Baked Salmon Provençal

2 tablespoons poly-unsaturated oil	1 8-ounce can tomato sauce
1 onion, chopped coarse	1 tablespoon lemon juice
1 stalk celery, chopped	½ teaspoon grated lemon peel
1 clove garlic, minced	¼ teaspoon basil
4 salmon steaks (1 to 1½ pounds)	1 green pepper, seeded and cut in julienne strips
½ teaspoon salt	
¼ teaspoon pepper	

Heat oil in a small skillet. Add onion, celery, and garlic. Sauté until the onion is golden, about 5 minutes.

Grease a shallow baking pan with special margarine (page 21). Place salmon steaks in the bottom of the pan and sprinkle with salt and pepper.

To the onion mixture in the skillet add tomato sauce, lemon juice, lemon peel, and basil. Mix well and pour over the salmon. Bake uncovered at 375°F. for 10 minutes. Add green pepper strips and bake an additional 15 minutes or until vegetables are tender and fish flakes easily with a fork. Serve with rice if desired. Serves 4.

Breaded Fillet of Sole

2 pounds fillet of sole
⅓ cup skim milk
½ small onion, minced
1½ cups fine bread crumbs
½ teaspoon paprika

¼ teaspoon parsley
2 tablespoons poly-
  unsaturated oil
2 small lemons, sliced
  thin

Preheat oven to 450°F.

Oil a shallow baking pan large enough so that all the fish can lie flat. Soak the fish in skim milk for 15 minutes. Combine minced onion and bread crumbs. Dip fish into bread crumb mixture until each piece is completely covered. Place fish in the greased pan. Sprinkle with paprika and dill. Dribble oil over all. Top with sliced lemon. Bake, uncovered, at 450°F. for 10 minutes. Serves 4.

Fillet of Flounder Senegalese

¾ cup fat-free cottage
  cheese
¼ cup mayonnaise
  (see page 56)

½ teaspoon curry powder
½ banana, puréed
2 pounds fillet of
  flounder, breaded

Preheat oven to 350°F. Combine cottage cheese, mayonnaise, curry powder, and banana. Place the fillets in a greased shallow baking dish large enough so that they can lie flat. Top each fillet with some of the curry mixture. Bake, uncovered, at 350°F. for 30 minutes. Serves 4.

Fish Frascati

1 pound fish fillets (any
  firm white-fleshed fish)
1 tablespoon minced
  parsley

1 teaspoon minced onion
  Salt and freshly ground
  pepper to taste
2 bananas, peeled

1½ tablespoons lemon juice	2 tablespoons special margarine (page 21)
1 tablespoon honey	3 tablespoons slivered almonds

Preheat oven to 400°F. Lay fish fillets in a shallow baking dish. Sprinkle parsley, onion, salt, and pepper over all.

Cut the bananas lengthwise in half and brush first with the lemon juice and then with the honey. Arrange in baking dish around fish. Sprinkle additional lemon juice over the fish. Dot with margarine and sprinkle with the almonds. Bake at 400°F. for 20 minutes or until fish flakes easily with a fork. Serves 3.

Shrimp Newburg

2 tablespoons special margarine (page 21)	1 13-ounce can (1⅔ cups) evaporated skim milk, at room temperature
1 tablespoon shallots, minced	
1 pound shrimp, washed, shelled, deveined, and cut in half vertically	¼ teaspoon prepared white horseradish
2 tablespoons flour	¾ cup frozen peas, defrosted

Melt margarine in a large skillet. Add shallots and shrimp and sauté until shrimp turns pink. Stir flour into the shrimp. When well mixed, remove from heat. Stir in the evaporated skim milk and the horseradish. Return to low heat and cook, stirring constantly, for 5 minutes. Add peas and keep stirring until sauce is thick enough to coat a spoon. Serve over rice. Serves 3 to 4.

Shrimp Scampi

¼ cup sesame seed oil	1 tablespoon lemon juice

2 garlic cloves, minced
½ teaspoon dill

2 pounds jumbo shrimp,
   washed, shelled, and
   deveined

Combine sesame seed oil, lemon juice, garlic, and dill in a
large glass bowl. Marinate shrimp in the mixture for two
hours at room temperature, turning the shrimp occasionally.
Pour the mixture and the shrimp into a large skillet and cook
until the shrimp turns pink. Transfer shrimp to a large platter
and serve with rice. Serves 4 to 5.

Sole Normand

2 pounds fillet of sole
   Salt and freshly ground
   pepper to taste
2 tablespoons special
   margarine (page 21)

12 cherry tomatoes, halved
1 cup mushrooms, sliced
1 onion, sliced and
   separated into rings
½ cup dry white wine
¾ teaspoon parsley flakes

Preheat oven to 400°F. Oil a large, shallow baking-to-table
dish. Arrange the fillet of sole in the dish. Season with salt
and pepper. Dot with margarine. Top fish with cherry tomatoes
(sliced-side-down), onion rings, and mushrooms. Pour wine
over all. Sprinkle with parsley flakes. Cover and bake at
400°F. for 10 minutes. Serves 4.

Sole Timbales

1 pound fillet of sole or
   other firm white-
   fleshed fish

1 medium tomato,
   peeled* and chopped

---

* To peel tomatoes easily, dip in boiling water for a few seconds. Remove
skin with a sharp knife.

4 tablespoons mayon-
naise (see page 56)
1 tablespoon poly-
unsaturated oil
1 small onion, chopped
fine
¼ cup celery, chopped
fine

½ cup ¼-inch bread
cubes
1 tablespoon minced
parsley
½ teaspoon basil
¼ teaspoon marjoram
Salt and freshly ground
pepper to taste

Grease 6 to 8 custard cups or the holes of muffin tins with
special margarine (page 21). Cut fillets in half lengthwise and
slice in 6-inch lengths. Spread 2 tablespoons of the mayonnaise over one side of each of the fillets. Place fillets, mayonnaise side down, over the bottom and sides of the custard
cups. Use small pieces of fish on the bottom. Set aside.

Heat oil in a small skillet. Sauté onion and celery 10
minutes. Stir in the chopped tomato, bread cubes, parsley,
basil, marjoram, salt, pepper, and the remaining 2 tablespoons
of mayonnaise. Fill each of the fish cups with some of the
mixture. Bake at 375°F. for 30 minutes or until fish flakes
easily with a fork. Serves 3.

Spaghetti with Red Clam Sauce

2 tablespoons poly-
unsaturated oil
2 cloves garlic, minced
1 8-ounce can minced
clams, drained with
liquid reserved
½ cup drained and
chopped canned
tomatoes
2 tablespoons liquid
from tomatoes

¼ cup tomato paste
¼ cup red wine
½ cup flat-leaf parsley,
finely chopped
½ teaspoon basil
½ teaspoon oregano
¾ teaspoon salt
¼ teaspoon pepper
1 pound spaghetti or
linguini, cooked
according to package
directions and drained

Heat oil in a heavy saucepan. Add garlic and sauté until garlic is lightly browned. Measure ½ cup of the reserved clam liquid and add to the skillet. Stir in tomatoes, tomato liquid, tomato paste, and wine. Bring to a boil. Cover and simmer over a low flame for 10 minutes.

Add parsley, basil, oregano, salt, and pepper to the saucepan. Mix well. Stir in clams. Simmer, covered, for 5 minutes. Pour over hot spaghetti, toss gently, and serve. Serves 2 to 4.

Steamed Sea Bass - Honan Style

3 Chinese mushrooms	1 2-pound sea bass
½ cup cooked rice	1 tablespoon white
2 scallions, minced	vinegar
1 tablespoon ginger,	½ teaspoon sugar
sliced very thin	1 tablespoon safflower
2 tablespoons dark soy	oil
sauce	¼ teaspoon pepper

Soak mushrooms in water to cover for 20 minutes. Drain (use liquid to cook rice or to add flavor to soups) and slice thin. Combine sliced mushrooms, rice, half the minced scallions, half the ginger, and 1 tablespoon soy sauce. Set aside.

Wash and clean the bass. Score lightly with a knife on both sides. Stuff bass with prepared rice mixture.

Bring water to boil in a steamer.* Mix remaining scallions and ginger with 1 tablespoon soy sauce, vinegar, sugar, safflower oil, and pepper. Place fish on a flameproof plate that will fit in steamer with an inch all around to spare (or use double thicknesses of foil). Pour soy sauce mixture over fish. Place in steamer. Cover and steam for 15 minutes or until fish flakes easily with a fork. Serves 2 to 3.

---

* If you don't own a steamer, improvise by using a large heavy pot or Dutch oven and 2 empty 8-ounce tomato sauce cans. Cut away top and bottom of cans and set them in water in the bottom of the pot. Put a pie plate or other heat-resistant plate on cans. Cover and steam as directed above.

Stuffed Flounder

1 medium onion, minced
4 slices white bread, cut into ¼-inch cubes
2 teaspoons parsley flakes
¼ cup polyunsaturated oil

4 1-pound whole flounders, cleaned (Remove backbones)
8 cherry tomatoes, quartered
Salt and freshly ground pepper to taste
Juice of 1 lemon

Preheat broiler. Combine minced onion, bread cubes, and 1 teaspoon parsley flakes. Sauté mixture in 1 tablespoon oil until the cubes are lightly browned. Stuff flounders loosely with the mixture. Combine cherry tomatoes with any remaining bread cube mixture and set aside. Place flounders in a well-oiled baking pan and season with salt and pepper. Pour lemon juice on the flounders. Brush with oil, reserving 1 tablespoon oil, and sprinkle with remaining 1 teaspoon parsley flakes. Broil on both sides until golden. One minute before flounder is done, sprinkle remaining bread cube-tomato mixture over fish. Dribble on the remaining 1 tablespoon oil and broil one minute or until tomatoes are warm and cubes are browned. Serves 4.

Sweet and Pungent Fish

¼ cup polyunsaturated oil
1 pound fish fillets (any firm, white-fleshed fish), cut up into 2-inch chunks
3 tablespoons brown sugar
2 tablespoons cornstarch
½ teaspoon salt
¼ teaspoon ground ginger

1 13¼-ounce can pineapple tidbits
3 tablespoons white vinegar
2 teaspoons soy sauce
⅓ cup chicken bouillon (or 1 bouillon cube dissolved in ⅓ cup water)
1 carrot, peeled
¼ cup water chestnuts, drained and sliced

| 1 onion, sliced into thin rings | 1 green pepper, seeded and cut into strips |
| | 2 tablespoons sherry |

Heat oil in a skillet. Add fish pieces and sauté 4 minutes per side or until fish flakes easily. Set aside in a warm place.

Mix brown sugar, cornstarch, salt, and ginger in a heavy saucepan. Drain pineapple tidbits and reserve liquid. Set tidbits aside. Add pineapple liquid, vinegar, soy sauce, and chicken bouillon to the sugar mixture. Cook, uncovered, over medium heat, stirring frequently, until mixture thickens and clears.

Cut the carrot into thirds lengthwise. Cut each carrot third lengthwise into thin slices. Add carrot slices, water chestnuts, and onion rings to the saucepan and simmer, uncovered, stirring occasionally, for 2 minutes. Add green pepper strips, pineapple tidbits, fish, and sherry and simmer, uncovered, for 2 minutes or until tender and warmed through. Serve over rice. Serves 3 to 4.

Tarragon Baked Shad

1 2-pound shad, boned and split	2 tablespoons poly-unsaturated oil
2 tablespoons special margarine (page 21)	Juice of 1 lemon
	½ teaspoon tarragon
	Salt and freshly ground pepper to taste

Preheat oven to 375°F. Grease a shallow baking pan. Place fish, skin side down, in the pan. In a small saucepan, combine margarine and oil and cook over a low flame until margarine melts. Add lemon juice and tarragon. Brush half the mixture onto fish. Season with salt and pepper. Bake 15 to 20 minutes, brushing occasionally with the remainder of the tarragon sauce, until the fish is lightly browned and flakes easily when tested with a fork. Serves 4.

Walnut Fish

2 tablespoons poly-
  unsaturated oil
1 clove garlic, minced
1 onion, chopped
⅓ cup crushed walnuts
  (process shelled nuts
  in blender at medium
  speed to crush)

½ cup cracker crumbs
½ teaspoon salt
¼ teaspoon curry powder
1 tablespoon lemon juice
1 pound fish fillets (any
  firm white-fleshed fish)
½ teaspoon paprika
⅓ cup white wine

Preheat oven to 350°F. Heat oil in a skillet. Add garlic and onion and sauté until onion is transparent. Turn off heat. Stir in crushed walnuts, cracker crumbs, salt, curry powder, and lemon juice.

Lay fish fillets on a flat surface. Divide walnut mixture evenly among the fillets. Roll up fillets around the stuffing and secure with string or toothpicks. Place in a shallow baking dish and sprinkle with paprika. Pour wine over all. Bake, uncovered, for 25 minutes in a 350°F. oven. Fish is done when it flakes easily with a fork. (Do not overcook.) Serves 3.

9

Vegetables

Since vegetables do not contain any cholesterol and have very little fat, they are an excellent choice for the low cholesterol gourmet. Vegetables are naturally delicious, so they don't require many fancy sauces. They are easy to cook, and they don't add an excessive number of calories. What could be better?

Do Not Use
   Butter
   Cream
   Hollandaise sauce
   Vegetables canned or frozen with butter or cream sauces
   Whole milk cheese sauces
   Whole milk

Do Use

All potatoes (white and sweet)
All rice and other grains
All vegetables, fresh, frozen, and canned, except those with
   butter or sauces added
Herbs and spices
Lemon juice, vinegar, and wine
Pastas, except egg noodles
Special margarine (page 21)

Helpful Hints

Do not overcook. Vegetables should be tender but crisp. Overcooking makes them soggy and causes vitamin loss.

Instead of butter, try lemon juice and one of your favorite herbs. Don't overseason. Vegetables have a wonderful taste of their own; they do not need much embellishment.

Red or white wines will heighten the taste of many vegetables. The white wines blend well with light colored vegetables; the red wines, with the darker green vegetables. Use only small amounts of wine (about 1 tablespoon for a serving of four).

Vegetables are crisp and delicious when prepared by the Chinese method: sauté vegetables in 1 to 2 teaspoons of polyunsaturated oil in a skillet or wok. Stir until all vegetables are very lightly coated. Cover and cook over low heat 5 to 10 minutes or until tender. Toss occasionally while cooking and add 1 teaspoon water if needed.

Another delicious way of preparing vegetables is by steaming. To steam, place vegetables on a rack in a pan containing just enough boiling water to generate steam (about ½ an inch). Cover the pan and steam until tender (adding more boiling water if needed). Steamed vegetables are especially good when covered with a few large leaves of moist lettuce during the steaming process.

Asparagus Vinaigrette

1 pound fresh asparagus   1 recipe vinaigrette
                                     sauce (page 58)

Slice off toughened portions of stem ends. Discard stem ends. Scrape off scales and tough outer skin with a vegetable peeler or sharp knife. Place asparagus in a large skillet and cover with boiling water. Cook, uncovered, for 10 minutes over medium heat. Let stand in water for 5 minutes away from heat before draining. Place in a shallow bowl and cover with vinaigrette sauce. Marinate in refrigerator at least 6 hours (or overnight). Turn occasionally. Serve cold or, if desired, warm up in the marinade over very low heat. Serves 4.

Asparagus with Capers

36 fresh asparagus (about 2½ pounds)
3 tablespoons special margarine (page 21)
¼ cup lemon juice
2 teaspoons caper liquid
2 tablespoons capers
Freshly ground pepper to taste

Wash asparagus in a large basin of cold water. Drain. Cut off the ends. Using a small knife or vegetable peeler, cut both sides of the stalk just to the tip to remove the tough outer skin of the stalk. Put asparagus in a heavy skillet with an inch of boiling water in the bottom. Cover tightly and cook 10 to 12 minutes. Drain, place on a warm platter, and cover with a clean cloth to keep warm. Melt margarine in a small saucepan. Add lemon juice, caper liquid, and capers. Simmer for one minute or until heated through. Pour sauce over the asparagus. Serves 6 to 8.

Broccoli with Horseradish Sauce

1 10-ounce package frozen broccoli spears
1½ tablespoons special margarine (page 21)
1½ tablespoons flour
½ cup skim milk
2 teaspoons prepared white horseradish
½ tablespoon lemon juice

Prepare broccoli according to package directions. Drain and set aside in a warm place.

Melt margarine in a saucepan over low heat. Do not brown. Stir in flour and cook over very low heat for 2 minutes. Add milk and cook, stirring, over low heat until thickened. Stir in horseradish and lemon juice. Pour over the warm broccoli spears and serve. Makes a generous ½ cup sauce. Serves 3.

Carrots Creole

1 cup carrots, peeled and sliced	1 bay leaf
¾ cup celery, sliced	⅛ teaspoon garlic powder
1 medium onion, chopped	¼ teaspoon thyme
1 8-ounce can tomatoes	Dash cayenne pepper (or more, according to taste)
½ teaspoon salt	½ cup water
¼ teaspoon pepper	¼ cup chopped green pepper
1 teaspoon sugar	

Place carrots, celery, onion, tomatoes and their liquid, salt, pepper, sugar, bay leaf, garlic powder, thyme, and cayenne pepper in a heavy saucepan. Mix well. Stir in water. Bring to a boil, cover, and simmer over low heat for 30 minutes. Add green pepper and simmer an additional 10 minutes. Discard bay leaf before serving. Serves 4.

Puréed Carrots

2 pounds carrots, scraped and cut into 1-inch pieces	2 tablespoons lemon juice
	1 teaspoon parsley, minced

Place carrots in boiling water to cover. Cover the pot and cook over moderate heat for 10 to 20 minutes, until tender.

Time depends on the size and age of the carrots. (Larger, older carrots will take longer.) Drain. Mash well with a potato masher. Place in blender container. Add lemon juice and process for 1 minute or until the carrots are well puréed. Add parsley and serve. Serves 4.

Vegetable Medley

3 stalks celery, sliced
4 carrots, peeled and
 sliced
1 onion, chopped coarse

1 cup beef stock
Salt and freshly ground
 pepper to taste
Dash sage

Place all the ingredients in a heavy saucepan. Cook, uncovered, over medium heat for 20 minutes or until all is tender and the stock is reduced. Stir occasionally. Serves 4.

Corn-on-the-Cob Deluxe

6 ears of corn, husks
 removed and ends
 broken off or trimmed
2 tablespoons sugar

⅓ cup special margarine
 (page 21)
1 tablespoon dill
Salt and freshly ground
 pepper to taste

Bring a large kettle of water to a boil. Add sugar. Drop corn into water. Return water to a boil and cook corn 3 more minutes. Do not overcook. Drain immediately. Cream margarine with dill. Add salt and pepper. Serve corn with a small dish of the creamed margarine. Serves 4 to 6.

Eggplant Casserole Deluxe

1 eggplant (about 1¼
 pounds)

¼ cup polyunsaturated oil
1 onion, chopped

1 stalk celery, chopped	1 green pepper, seeded and chopped
1 clove garlic, minced	¼ pound fresh mush- rooms, cut in thirds vertically
1 teaspoon salt	
¼ teaspoon pepper	
½ teaspoon basil	
¼ teaspoon oregano	1 tablespoon minced parsley
2 tablespoons red wine	
2 tablespoons tomato paste	1 pound spaghetti or vermicelli, cooked according to package directions and drained
1 15-ounce can tomato sauce	
	2 tablespoons bread crumbs

Preheat oven to 350°F. Wash eggplant but do not peel. Cut off stem end. Cut into ½-inch cubes by slicing eggplant into ½-inch horizontal slices and cutting vertically at ½-inch intervals.

Heat oil in a large skillet or Dutch oven. Add eggplant cubes, onion, celery, and garlic and sauté until the onion is translucent and eggplant is lightly browned. Add salt, pepper, basil, oregano, wine, tomato paste, and tomato sauce. Stir to mix well. Bring to a boil, cover, and simmer over low heat for 10 minutes. Stir in green pepper, mushrooms, and parsley. Cover again and simmer another 5 minutes.

Grease a casserole dish with corn oil margarine and layer half the cooked spaghetti over the bottom. Top with half the eggplant mixture. Cover with another layer of spaghetti and another of eggplant. Sprinkle bread crumbs over all. Bake, uncovered, at 350°F. for 20 minutes. Serves 3 to 4 as a main dish, 6 to 8 as a side dish.

Fancy Green Beans

1 9-ounce package frozen whole green beans	1 tablespoon sesame seed or safflower oil

1 onion, chopped fine	Salt and freshly ground
½ teaspoon Worcester-	pepper to taste
shire sauce	¼ teaspoon thyme

Defrost beans. Heat oil in a heavy skillet and sauté onion until golden. Add the green beans and stir until beans are coated with a thin layer of onion mixture. Add the Worcestershire sauce. Cover and cook for 3 to 5 minutes or until the beans are heated through. Stir occasionally to prevent sticking. Season with salt and pepper. Just before serving, sprinkle with thyme. Serves 3.

Green Beans with Pimiento

1 pound fresh green beans	1 onion, sliced and separated into rings
1 tablespoon special margarine (page 21)	1 whole pimiento, cut into thin strips
	Salt and freshly ground pepper to taste

Wash the beans in cold water and snap off the ends. Bring a large kettle of salted water to a boil. Drop in the beans and cook 6 to 7 minutes. (Taste one bean. They should be tender but crisp. Do not overcook.) Drain in a colander. (Cooking liquid, which contains many vegetable minerals, can be saved and used in soup stock.) In a medium-sized skillet, melt the margarine. Sauté the onion until transparent. Add the beans and pimiento slices and toss 1 minute over medium heat. Season with salt and freshly ground pepper. Serves 4.

Tarragon Green Beans

1 pound green beans, washed	1 teaspoon sesame seed oil

½ teaspoon tarragon   Salt and freshly ground
                                       pepper to taste

Bring a large kettle of salted water to a boil. Snap off ends
of beans and drop beans into water. Bring the water back
to a boil. Reduce heat and cook beans 8 to 10 minutes or
until tender. Drain immediately into a colander. (Save liquid
for soup stock.) Run cold water on the beans to preserve their
color. Just before serving, add sesame seed oil to a skillet.
Toss the beans to prevent sticking and cook until they are
lightly coated and heated through. Sprinkle with tarragon
and season with salt and pepper. Serves 3 to 4.

Sautéed Mushrooms

2 tablespoons special   8 cherry tomatoes, cut
  margarine (page 21)   in half
1 onion, chopped   ¼ teaspoon dill
1½ cups small mushrooms,   Salt and freshly ground
  cut in half   pepper to taste

Melt margarine in a small skillet. Add onion and sauté until
transparent. Add mushrooms and sauté until they are lightly
browned. Add cherry tomatoes and sauté until they are just
heated through but still crisp. Sprinkle with dill and season
with salt and pepper. Serves 2.

Vermicelli with Mushrooms

1 8-ounce package   1½ cups mushrooms,
  vermicelli   sliced
¼ cup sesame seed oil   1 garlic clove, minced
2 tablespoons special   1 teaspoon parsley flakes
  margarine (page 21)   Salt and freshly ground
                                     pepper to taste

Bring a large kettle of salted water to a boil. Drop in vermicelli and cook 10 to 12 minutes or to desired tenderness, stirring occasionally. Drain and place in a serving bowl. Put oil and margarine in a small skillet over low heat. When margarine has melted, add mushrooms and garlic, stirring occasionally, until the mushrooms are tender (about 10 minutes). Pour over the vermicelli, sprinkle with parsley, and season with salt and pepper. Serves 4.

Potato Sticks

6 medium potatoes,
washed and peeled
¼ cup polyunsaturated oil

½ teaspoon paprika
1 teaspoon parsley flakes
Salt and freshly ground
pepper to taste

Preheat broiler. Cut each potato into thirds horizontally and then into strips. Soak sticks in cold, salted water for 15 minutes. Drain and pat dry. Put on a large cookie sheet. Pour on oil and toss potatoes until they are lightly coated. Sprinkle with paprika and parsley. Season with salt and freshly ground pepper. Broil for 15 minutes, turning occasionally, until potatoes are brown and tender. Serves 4.

Madrid Rice

2 tablespoons special
margarine (page 21)
1 onion, chopped
1 cup converted rice
2½ cups chicken bouillon

⅛ teaspoon saffron
⅛ teaspoon salt
1 cup frozen peas
1 whole pimiento, seeded
and cut into strips

Melt margarine in a large skillet. Sauté chopped onion in margarine. When onion is transparent, reduce heat and add rice. Continue to sauté. When rice is golden, add the chicken bouillon and saffron. Cover and cook 20 minutes or until most of the water is absorbed. Season with salt. Stir in peas and cook, covered, 5 more minutes. Add the pimiento strips and cook, uncovered, until all the liquid is absorbed. Serves 6.

Orange Rice

1½ tablespoons special
    margarine (page 21)
1 onion, chopped
1 cup converted rice

1 teaspoon salt
1 11-ounce can mandarin
   oranges in light syrup
2 cups water

Melt margarine in a heavy skillet. Add onion and sauté until onion is transparent. Add rice and salt and continue to sauté until rice is golden. Drain oranges, reserving syrup. Measure syrup and, if necessary, add enough water to make ½ cup. Add syrup and the two cups of water to rice. Cover tightly and cook over low heat until almost all the liquid is absorbed and rice is tender. Stir mandarin oranges into rice. Cover and cook 2 to 3 more minutes or until heated through. Serves 5 to 6.

Juniper Kraut

2 tablespoons poly-
   unsaturated oil
1 onion, chopped
1 1-pound package
   sauerkraut, drained

1 tablespoon juniper
   berries
¼ cup sauerkraut liquid
3 tablespoons tomato
   juice
1 tablespoon sugar

Heat oil in a skillet that has a cover. Add onion and sauté until golden, about 5 minutes. Stir in sauerkraut, juniper berries, sauerkraut liquid, tomato juice, and sugar. Mix well.

Bring to a boil, cover, and simmer for 10 minutes. Serve with broiled hamburgers, lamb chops, veal chops, or steak. Serves 4 to 6.

Puréed Spinach

2 pounds fresh spinach
2 tablespoons special margarine (page 21)

2 tablespoons lemon juice
Sprinkling of nutmeg to taste

Tear off the stems of the spinach. Put in a colander and wash well. Place the spinach, with just the water that adheres to the leaves after washing, in a stainless steel kettle.° Cook over medium heat until spinach wilts (3 to 5 minutes), stirring occasionally. Cool slightly. Put spinach, margarine, lemon juice, and nutmeg in the blender container. Process until puréed. Put back in the kettle just to heat through. Serve in a warm enamel or porcelain bowl.°° Serves 4.

Baked Acorn Squash With Honey

2 acorn squash, cut in half (remove seeds)
2 tablespoons special margarine, melted (page 21)

4 teaspoons honey
⅛ teaspoon cinnamon

Preheat oven to 400°F. Line a baking sheet with aluminum foil. Brush each squash half, both cavity and rim, with 1

° When cooking spinach, do not use an iron or aluminum kettle. These metals can cause spinach to have a metallic taste.
°° Do not serve spinach in a silver bowl. Silver can also cause spinach to pick up a metallic taste.

teaspoon melted margarine. Cover tightly with aluminum foil and bake at 400°F. for 25 minutes or until tender when pierced with a fork. Brush with remaining margarine. Add 1 teaspoon honey and a sprinkling of cinnamon to each cavity. Continue baking, uncovered, until lightly browned, about 5 to 10 minutes. Serves 4.

Stuffed Tomatoes

6 large beefsteak tomatoes	1 small onion, minced fine
½ teaspoon salt	¼ pound fresh mushrooms, minced fine
½ cup fine white bread crumbs	¼ teaspoon thyme
2½ tablespoons polyunsaturated oil	½ teaspoon oregano Freshly ground pepper to taste

Preheat oven to 375°F. Cut each tomato in half crosswise. Gently press out the juice and seeds from the tomatoes into a medium-sized glass mixing bowl. Using a small knife, cut out the pulp. (Be careful not to cut into the tomato shell.) Salt the tomato shells. Turn them over and let them drain. Chop the pulp. Add pulp and the bread crumbs to the tomato juice and seeds. Sauté the minced onion and minced mushrooms in 1 tablespoon oil until lightly browned. Sprinkle with thyme. Add onions and mushrooms to the bread crumb-tomato mixture. Put tomatoes in an oiled shallow roasting pan. Fill each shell with the mixture. Sprinkle with oregano and freshly ground pepper. Dribble remaining 1½ tablespoons of oil over the top of the tomatoes. Bake at 375°F. for 15 minutes. Place under the broiler until the filling is lightly browned on top. Serves 6.

Lemon Zucchini

1 pound zucchini,
  washed but unpeeled
3 tablespoons poly-
  unsaturated oil
2 onions, chopped fine
1 clove garlic, minced
½ green pepper, seeded
  and cut in julienne strips

½ teaspoon basil
2 tablespoons pine nuts
3 tablespoons lemon
  juice
2½ teaspoons minced
  parsley
Salt and pepper to taste

Cut zucchini in half horizontally. Slice each half in eighths lengthwise. Set aside.

Heat oil in a heavy skillet. Add zucchini, onions, and garlic and sauté until the onion is transparent and the zucchini is lightly browned on all sides (about 5 minutes). Add green pepper strips, basil, and pine nuts. Sauté 2 minutes or until green pepper is crisp but tender. Stir in lemon juice, parsley, salt, and pepper. Simmer 1 minute. Serve hot or cold. Serves 4.

Stuffed Zucchini

4 large zucchini, about
  1½ pounds
½ teaspoon salt
¾ cup fine rye bread
  crumbs
6 cherry tomatoes or 2
  medium tomatoes,
  chopped fine

1 shallot, minced
½ teaspoon oregano
2 tablespoons poly-
  unsaturated oil
  Freshly ground pepper
  to taste

Preheat oven to 350°F. Wash zucchini and trim the ends. Put zucchini in a large kettle of boiling water and cook for 10 minutes or until tender when pressed. Remove from water and cut in half lengthwise. Using a spoon, carefully hollow out the pulp of the zucchini. Chop the pulp and set aside. Salt each shell. Turn shells over and let them drain. Mix rye bread crumbs, chopped tomatoes, minced shallot, and oregano. Add zucchini pulp. Grease a shallow baking pan. Put zucchini shells in the pan and stuff with the bread crumb mixture. Season with pepper. Pour oil evenly over each stuffed zucchini. Bake at 350°F. for 30 minutes. Serves 4.

Zucchini in Red Wine

3 tablespoons poly-unsaturated oil

1 pound zucchini, washed, unpeeled, and sliced ½ inch thick

1 medium onion, chopped

1 clove garlic, minced

¼ pound mushrooms, sliced in thirds vertically

¼ teaspoon thyme

¼ cup dry red wine

Heat the oil in a heavy skillet. Add zucchini, onion, and garlic and sauté over medium heat, turning often, until zucchini is lightly browned on both sides and onion is golden (about 3 to 5 minutes). Add mushrooms and thyme. Sauté for 2 more minutes or until zucchini is crisply tender. Add the wine. Cook, stirring, over medium heat until wine is somewhat reduced, about 1 minute. Serves 4.

10

Desserts

Rich desserts tempt everyone—even the low cholesterol gourmet. However, you *can* have your cake and eat it too. Although there is a large "do not use" list, this certainly doesn't mean you have to give up all of your favorite desserts. Fudgy-rich chocolate cake, smooth coffee ice cream, old-fashioned apple pie, and elegant chocolate mousse can be part of your low cholesterol eating plan.

Do Not Use
  Butter
  Chocolate
  Coconut
  Commercial cookies and other baked goods
  Commercial ice cream

Commercial products made with coconut or palm oil
Cream cheese or whole milk ricotta cheese
Egg yolk or whole egg (unless part of weekly egg allotment)
Hydrogenated fats, such as Crisco or Spry
Light or heavy cream
Whole milk

Do Use
All flour
All fruit (except avocado)
All gelatins, flavored and unflavored
All sugar, brown, confectioners, and granulated
All wines and liqueurs
Baking powder and soda
Cocoa
Cornstarch
Egg white
Evaporated skim milk
Safflower oil
Sherbet
Special margarine, sweet and salted (page 21)

Helpful Hints
To convert your own favorite desserts to low cholesterol desserts, try substituting polyunsaturated vegetable oils (safflower has the most delicate flavor) for hydrogenated vegetable oils such as Crisco or Spry. Allow ¾ cup oil for each cup of solid fat.

You can sometimes substitute 1 egg white for 1 egg yolk, 2 egg whites for 1 whole egg, or 3 egg whites for 2 eggs. When using the recipes in this book, however, follow them without substitution. The use of yolks has already been minimized as much as possible.

To substitute for bitter chocolate, you can use 2½ tablespoons of cocoa and 1½ teaspoons safflower oil for each ounce of bitter chocolate.

When beating egg whites, make sure that the bowl and beaters are absolutely clean. A tiny bit of grease can prevent the whites from peaking properly. If possible, beat whites in a copper bowl; the chemical reaction between the egg whites and the copper will allow the greatest amount of air to be incorporated into the beaten whites. Substitute porcelain, glass, or steel bowls if a copper one is not available but never beat whites in a plastic bowl. Egg whites are well whipped if they stand in stiff peaks when the beaters or whisk are raised.

Applesauce Cake

10 graham crackers, crushed (1⅓ cups)
1¼ cups flour
1½ teaspoon salt
1 tablespoon baking soda
1¾ cups applesauce (15-ounce jar)
3 tablespoons fresh lemon juice

2 teaspoons lemon rind, finely grated
2 eggs, separated
1 cup sugar
⅓ cup nonfat dry milk dissolved in ⅔ cup water
2 teaspoons cinnamon
Scant ½ teaspoon nutmeg
1 teaspoon vanilla

Preheat oven to 350°F. Spread ⅔ cup of the graham cracker crumbs over bottom of a 10-inch (4 inches deep) spring form tube pan (angel food pan). Set aside.

Sift flour, salt, and baking soda together. Set aside.

Combine applesauce, lemon juice, and lemon rind. Set aside.

Beat egg yolks slightly. Gradually add sugar, beating constantly in an electric mixer until mixture is thick and lemon colored. Beat in milk, cinnamon, nutmeg, and vanilla. Add the applesauce mixture alternately with the flour mixture.

Beat egg whites until they form stiff peaks. Fold into the applesauce mixture. Turn into the spring form pan and top with the remaining ⅔ cup crumbs. Spread crumbs evenly and press them slightly into the batter. Bake at 350°F. for 45 minutes or until a toothpick inserted near the center of the cake comes out clean. Serve this rich, moist cake alone or topped with lemon sherbet. Serves 12 to 14.

Charlotte's Chocolate Cake

1 stick (¼ pound) special
   margarine (page 21)
2 cups sugar
2 eggs, separated
1¾ cups flour
1 teaspoon baking
   powder

⅔ cup cocoa
1 cup skim milk
1 tablespoon black
   coffee
1 teaspoon vanilla
½ teaspoon almond
   extract

Preheat oven to 325°F. Grease a 9-inch spring form cake pan with special margarine.

In the bowl of an electric mixer cream margarine and sugar. Beat in egg yolks, 1 at a time. Sift flour and baking powder together. Add approximately ⅓ of the flour mixture to the egg yolk mixture. Then add approximately ⅓ of the cocoa and ⅓ of the milk. Repeat until all ingredients are used up, ending with the milk. Beat in coffee, vanilla, and almond extract. Clean beaters and beat egg whites until they stand in stiff peaks. Fold into the batter gently. Pour batter into the prepared cake pan. Bake at 325°F. for 45 minutes or until a toothpick inserted into the cake comes out clean. Let cool before serving. Serves 10.

Cheesecake

1 pound neufchatel
   cheese, softened
1 cup low-fat cottage
   cheese
¾ cup sugar
2 eggs, separated
2 tablespoons cornstarch

2 tablespoons flour
   Dash salt
½ cup nonfat dry milk dissolved in 1¼ cups
   water
1 teaspoon vanilla
3 tablespoons fresh
   lemon juice

Preheat oven to 325°F. Beat softened neufchatel cheese and cottage cheese together at high speed with an electric mixer until smooth. Beat in the sugar. When ingredients are well mixed, beat in the egg yolks. Beat in the cornstarch, flour, and salt at medium speed. Beat in milk, vanilla, and lemon juice.

Beat the egg whites until stiff peaks form. Fold gently into the cheese mixture. Grease an 8- or 9-inch spring form pan with special margarine (page 21). Pour in batter. Bake at 325°F. for 1 hour and 10 minutes. Turn off heat. Let cake sit in oven for 2 hours without opening oven door. Remove from oven and let cool to room temperature before removing spring form. Chill in refrigerator before serving. Serves 10 to 12.

Cocoa Cookies

Cocoa mix:

5 tablespoons cocoa	1 tablespoon safflower oil
	2 teaspoons water

Batter:

1 egg	1¾ cup sifted all-purpose flour
2 egg whites	
½ cup safflower oil	½ teaspoon baking soda
1 teaspoon vanilla	½ teaspoon baking powder
¾ cup sugar	½ teaspoon salt
	2 teaspoons rum

Preheat oven to 375°F. Place cocoa, oil, and water in a small saucepan. Cook over low heat, stirring constantly, until cocoa is melted. Remove from heat.

Combine the egg and egg whites in a large bowl. Beat well. Beat in oil and vanilla. Blend in sugar. Sift dry ingredients together and add. Mix well until a smooth batter is formed. Stir in melted cocoa, stirring until batter is a chocolate color. Stir in the rum. Drop the cookies from a teaspoon onto a greased cookie sheet. Bake at 375°F. for 10 minutes. Makes 4 dozen.

Wheat Germ Balls

½ cup sweet special
   margarine (page 21)
1 cup sugar
1 egg
1 teaspoon vanilla
½ teaspoon baking
   powder

¼ teaspoon salt
2 cups sifted all-purpose
   flour
¼ cup wheat germ
4 teaspoons skim milk
½ teaspoon cinnamon

Preheat oven to 400°F. Cream margarine and blend in sugar. Mix in egg and vanilla. Sift together baking powder, salt, and flour and stir into mixture. Add wheat germ, skim milk, and cinnamon. Mix well. Shape into 1-inch diameter balls and place on a greased cookie sheet. Bake at 400°F. for 10 minutes. Makes 4 dozen.

Apple Pie

2½ pounds apples
½ cup sugar
   Dash salt
   Pastry for a 9-inch
   double crust pie (page
   136)
¼ cup honey

¼ teaspoon allspice
½ teaspoon cinnamon
2 tablespoons lemon
   juice
1 tablespoon special
   margarine (page 21)

Pare and core apples. Cut each apple into quarters; then cut each quarter into thirds. Set aside.

Preheat oven to 425°F.

Mix sugar and salt. Line a 9-inch pie pan with pastry and sprinkle 2 tablespoons of the sugar mixture over the bottom. Mix apple slices with the remaining sugar. Stir in the honey gently. Arrange apple slices over the pastry. Sprinkle on allspice, cinnamon, and lemon juice. Dot with margarine. Put on top crust. Make small gashes in top crust to allow steam to escape. Seal edges, according to the directions on page 137. Place on the middle shelf of oven and bake at 425°F. for 15 minutes. Lower the heat to 350°F. and bake an additional 30 minutes. Cool before serving. Serves 8.

Chocolate Chiffon Pie

1 egg yolk
Dash salt
3 tablespoons strong black coffee
1 tablespoon coffee liqueur
⅓ cup cocoa
1 tablespoon special margarine (page 21)
½ cup plus 1 tablespoon sugar
¼ cup nonfat dry milk dissolved in ½ cup hot tap water
1 ¼-ounce envelope (1 tablespoon) unflavored gelatin
¼ cup cold water
1 teaspoon vanilla
¼ teaspoon almond extract
3 egg whites
1 9-inch single-crust baked pie shell

Combine egg yolk, salt, black coffee, coffee liqueur, cocoa, and special margarine in the top of a double boiler. Cook over slowly boiling water for 2 minutes, stirring constantly.

Stir in sugar and milk. Cook, stirring constantly, over slowly boiling water for 3 minutes. Remove from heat and let cool.

Soften the gelatin in the cold water. Cook over low heat until dissolved. Stir the gelatin, vanilla, and almond extract into the cocoa mixture.

Beat egg whites until they stand in fairly stiff peaks. Fold egg whites gently into the cocoa mixture. Pour into the prepared pie shell. Chill in refrigerator until set. Serves 8.

Fresh Peach Pie

2 pounds ripe peaches
1 cup sugar
  Dash salt
½ teaspoon cinnamon
  Dash nutmeg
2 teaspoons cornstarch
1 tablespoon flour

¼ teaspoon almond
  extract
1 tablespoon special
  margarine (page 21)
  Pastry for a 9-inch
  double-crust pie

Preheat oven to 450°F. Peel the peaches, and cut them in half. Remove pits. Cut each half into quarters vertically. Measure the slices (there should be 3½ to 4 cups). Set aside.

Mix together the sugar, salt, cinnamon, nutmeg, cornstarch, and flour. Add the peaches and mix gently until all the peaches are coated with the mixture. Stir in almond extract.

Line a pie plate with pastry according to directions on page 137. Spread peach mixture over pastry and dot with the special margarine. Cover with the top crust. Bake at 450°F. for 15 minutes. Lower oven heat to 350°F and bake an additional 25 minutes. Serves 8.

Pie Crust No. 1 – Special Margarine

2 cups sifted all-purpose
  flour
1 teaspoon salt

⅔ cup plus 1 tablespoon
  special margarine
  (page 21)
6 tablespoons cool
  (not ice) water

Sift flour and salt together into a mixing bowl. Cut ⅓ cup of the margarine into the flour mixture with a pastry blender. (If you don't own a pastry blender, a wire whisk works well. Grasp the whisk firmly and pound gently.) The mixture should look like coarse cornmeal. Add the remaining margarine, cutting it into the dough until it is the size of large peas.

Sprinkle on the water, tossing mixture lightly with a fork. Gently press dough together with the hands until it forms a ball. Cover bowl and refrigerate for 10 minutes.

Divide dough into 2 slightly uneven portions. Roll the larger section with a floured rolling pin until it is ⅛ inch thick and overlaps pie plate by half an inch. Fold in half and use a pancake turner or cleaver to transfer to the bottom of a 9-inch pie plate. Unfold dough in the pan and gently press over the bottom and sides of the pie pan, letting edges overhang. Fill with desired filling.

Roll out top crust with floured rolling pin, fold in half, and transfer to pie. Unfold and press down edges at rim of pie plate. Trim overhanging edges with a sharp knife. Press the rim of the pie plate with the tines of a fork to flute edges. Using a small sharp knife, make several gashes in the top crust to allow steam to escape. Bake according to filling directions.

To make a lattice crust, roll out top pastry and cut into ½-inch strips. Interweave strips on top of pie. Press edges down as directed above.

To make only a bottom crust, divide recipe in half.

If a baked crust is desired (for fillings that need no baking), bake at 425°F. for 15 to 20 minutes. Let cool before filling.

Makes pastry for a double-crust 9-inch pie.

Pie Crust No. 2 – Oil

2 cups plus 2 tablespoons sifted all-purpose flour	2 teaspoons salt
	½ cup safflower oil
	⅓ cup ice-cold skim milk

Sift the flour and salt together into a mixing bowl. Mix oil and milk. Pour all at once over the flour and mix well with a fork. When blended, shape into a ball and divide into 2 slightly uneven parts. Roll the larger part between 2 sheets of waxed paper until it is about 1½ inches larger all around than a

9-inch pie plate. Remove top layer of waxed paper, and invert pie plate over dough. Using the waxed paper edges, flip dough and pie plate over. Press dough gently into pie plate, trim edges, and fill with desired filling.

Roll out remaining ball of dough between 2 sheets of waxed paper. Remove top sheet. Using the edges of the waxed paper, flip dough onto filled pie. Cut gashes in top crust to allow steam to escape. Flute edges. Bake according to filling directions.

To make only a bottom crust, cut recipe in half.

If a baked crust is desired (for fillings that need no baking), bake at 450°F. for 15 to 20 minutes. Let cool before filling.

Makes pastry for a double-crust 9-inch pie.

Pie Crust No. 3 – Graham Cracker

10 graham crackers, crushed (1⅓ cups)°
¼ cup sugar
¼ teaspoon salt

Dash cinnamon (optional)
5 tablespoons special margarine, melted (page 21)

Mix graham cracker crumbs, sugar, salt, and cinnamon together. Stir in melted margarine and mix until crumbs are moistened. Press mixture over the bottom and sides of a 9-inch pie pan. Bake 10 minutes at 350°F. Cool before filling. Makes 1 9-inch single crust.

Burgundy Strawberries

1 quart strawberries, washed and hulled

3½ cups Burgundy wine
1 cup sugar

° Honey graham or cinnamon and sugar graham crackers may be used in place of plain graham crackers.

2 teaspoons lemon juice
1½ cinnamon sticks

½ teaspoon orange rind,
cut in julienne strips

Prick each strawberry several times with a fork and place in a large glass serving bowl. Combine Burgundy wine, sugar, lemon juice, cinnamon sticks, and orange rind in a saucepan. Cook over moderate heat, stirring occasionally, until mixture just begins to boil. Pour over the strawberries. Chill 4 hours or more. Serves 4.

Strawberry Rhubarb

¾ pound rhubarb stalks,
  cut into 1-inch pieces
1 pound strawberries
  (1 dry pint), washed
  and hulled
2 tablespoons orange
  juice

¾ cup honey
1 tablespoon sugar
1 teaspoon cornstarch
4 strawberries, halved
  Confectioners sugar to
  taste

Combine rhubarb, 1 pound strawberries, orange juice, and honey in a medium-sized saucepan. Cover and cook over low heat for 10 minutes or until strawberries and rhubarb are partially dissolved. Add sugar and cornstarch and cook, uncovered, stirring constantly, for 5 minutes or until mixture has slightly thickened. Chill and serve topped with halved strawberries and a sprinkling of confectioners sugar. Serves 4 to 6.

Coffee Ice Cream

¾ cup nonfat dry milk
1 cup evaporated skim
  milk

¼ cup safflower oil
1 teaspoon instant coffee
  powder

1 teaspoon cocoa
2 tablespoons confec-
tioners sugar

½ teaspoon coffee
liqueur

Put nonfat dry milk and evaporated skim milk in blender container. Process at high speed for 1 minute. Continue blending and slowly add the safflower oil. Add all remaining ingredients. Process at high speed for 1 minute. Pour into individual dessert dishes or freezer tray. Cover and freeze. Serves 4.

Chocolate Mousse

¼ cup cocoa
½ cup sugar
1 tablespoon safflower
oil
3 tablespoons water
1 teaspoon vanilla

⅛ teaspoon cinnamon
2 eggs
1⅔ cups evaporated skim
milk (1 13-oz. can)
1 teaspoon instant coffee
powder

Preheat oven to 325°F. Mix cocoa and sugar in a small saucepan. Add oil, water, vanilla, and cinnamon. Cook over low heat, stirring constantly, until cocoa mixture is melted and smooth. Pour into blender container.

Add eggs. Cover and blend on lowest speed for 30 seconds. Add evaporated skim milk and coffee powder and continue to blend for 20 seconds. Pour into a soufflé dish or into individual baking dishes. Place in a shallow pan containing 1 inch of hot water. Bake at 325°F. for 45 minutes or until a toothpick inserted in the middle comes out clean. Serves 4.

Lemon Chiffon Pudding

1 ¼-ounce envelope
unflavored gelatin
¼ cup cold water

2 egg yolks
⅔ cup sugar
Juice of 2 lemons

Grated peel of ½ lemon
1 tablespoon safflower
   oil

4 egg whites
8 fresh strawberries,
   washed and hulled

Put gelatin and cold water in a metal measuring cup. Half-fill a small skillet with water. Heat water and place the cup in the skillet until the gelatin is dissolved. Put egg yolk and sugar in a large mixing bowl. Beat until the yolk has completely adhered to all the sugar. Add lemon juice, grated lemon peel, safflower oil, and dissolved gelatin. Beat well until mixture is slightly thickened. Set aside.

Beat egg whites in a deep bowl until stiff. Fold egg whites into the lemon mixture. Refrigerate. Serve well chilled and garnish with fresh strawberries. Serves 4.

Old-Fashioned Rice Pudding

2 cups cooked rice
½ cup water
1 cup skim milk
1 cup evaporated skim
   milk
1 egg, at room
   temperature

2 egg whites, at room
   temperature
⅓ cup sugar
1 teaspoon vanilla
¼ cup raisins, washed
1 11-ounce can Mandarin
   oranges, drained
¼ teaspoon cinnamon

Preheat oven to 350°F. Place cooked rice in a large saucepan. Add water. Cover and simmer until all water is absorbed (2 to 3 minutes). Add skim milk and evaporated skim milk. Stir until mixture comes to a gentle boil and thickens (5 to 10 minutes). Remove from heat. Combine egg, egg whites, sugar, and vanilla in a large bowl. Beat well. Slowly add the milk-rice mixture. Mix well. Add raisins, Mandarin oranges, and cinnamon. Pour into a 1½-quart greased casserole. Place the casserole in a pan containing one inch of hot water. Bake at 350°F. for 45 minutes or until a toothpick inserted in the middle comes out clean. Serve warm or chilled. Serves 6 to 8.

Raspberry Parfait

Juice of 1 lime
1 envelope plain gelatin
½ cup boiling water
2 egg whites

1 10-ounce package
  frozen raspberries,
  defrosted
2 teaspoons red currant
  jelly

Put lime juice, gelatin, and boiling water into a blender container. Process at low speed for 30 seconds. Add egg whites and process at high speed for 30 seconds. Add frozen raspberries (with their juice) and the jelly and process at high speed for 15 seconds. Pour into individual serving glasses. Serves 4.

Susan Fraser's Orange Freeze

2 3-ounce packages
  orange gelatin
2 cups boiling water
1½ cups cold water

1 11-ounce can Mandarin
  oranges
1 pint orange sherbet,
  softened

Add orange gelatin to the boiling water and stir until dissolved. Turn into a large mixing bowl and stir in the cold water. Drain oranges, reserving ¼ cup syrup. Add syrup to the gelatin mixture and stir well. Chill in refrigerator until mixture is very soft and syrupy (about 1 to 1½ hours). Add the sherbet and beat with an electric mixer until well mixed. Fold in the drained orange sections and turn into a 1½-quart mold. Chill until firm. Serves 8.

Café Hot Fudge Sauce

⅓ cup cocoa
⅔ cup sugar

1 teaspoon instant coffee
  powder

1 tablespoon poly-
   unsaturated oil

¼ cup water
¼ cup evaporated skim
   milk

Mix cocoa, sugar, and coffee powder in a saucepan. Add oil and water. Cook over low heat, stirring constantly, until cocoa mixture is completely dissolved. Add evaporated skim milk and continue stirring until the sauce is heated through and smooth. Makes 1 cup.

11

Fat and Cholesterol Content of Common Foods

Counting grams and milligrams will help you keep cholesterol and saturated fat intake to acceptable levels. Cholesterol intake should be limited to 300 milligrams per day. Saturated fat intake should be limited to approximately 11 percent of the body's total caloric intake. Monounsaturated (oleic) fat and polyunsaturated (linoleic) fat should account for approximately another 11 percent each. (See page 16 for help in calculating saturated fat.)

The following chart has been compiled from statistical information contained in *Nutritive Value of Foods*, U.S. Department of Agriculture, Home and Garden Bulletin No. 72, and *Composition of Foods*, Agriculture Handbook No. 8, U.S. Department of Agriculture.

Dashes (—) indicate that no suitable value has been officially assigned to the item under consideration but there is reason to believe that a measurable amount may be present. A plus (+) next to a number indicates that while the value has not been officially assigned, it is known to be *above* the number indicated. A curved sign (~) indicates an approximation. The standard measurement used in the chart is 100 grams (3½ ounces). Unless a different measurement is next to an item in the chart, the fat and cholesterol figures are for 100 grams of the item.

Product	Saturated Fat (grams)	Mono-unsaturated (Oleic) Fatty Acid (grams)	Poly-unsaturated (Linoleic) Fatty Acid (grams)	Cholesterol (milligrams)
Almonds (see *Nuts*)				
Apple, 1 medium	—	—	—	0
Apple juice, 1 cup	—	—	—	0
Applesauce, 1 cup				
canned	—	—	—	0
Apricots, 3 raw	—	—	—	0
Asparagus, 4 spears	—	—	—	0
Avocados, whole raw				
California, 1 medium	7	17	5	0
Florida, 1 medium	7	15	4	0
Banana, 1 medium	—	—	—	0
Bacon, broiled or fried,				
drained	17	25	5	~70
2 slices	3	4	1	~26
Bacon, Canadian	5	6	1	~70
Beans, 1 cup cooked				
and drained				
lima, immature seeds	—	—	—	0
green	—	—	—	0
yellow or wax	—	—	—	0
Beans, 1 cup dry				
Navy (pea) cooked				
and drained	—	—	—	0
Red kidney, canned	—	—	—	0
Beechnuts (see *Nuts*)				

Product	Saturated Fat (grams)	Mono-unsaturated (Oleic) Fatty Acid (grams)	Poly-unsaturated (Linoleic) Fatty Acid (grams)	Cholesterol (milligrams)
Beef, raw				
hamburger				
regular	10	9	trace	70
lean	5	4	trace	70
porterhouse	17	16	1	70
rib roast				
untrimmed	18	16	1	70
trimmed	6	5	trace	70
round				
untrimmed	6	5	trace	70
trimmed	2	2	trace	70
sirloin	14	13	1	70
Beer, 12 fl oz	—	—	—	0
Beets, 1 cup canned	—	—	—	0
Blackberries, 1 cup raw	—	—	—	0
Blueberries, 1 cup raw	—	—	—	0
Bluefish	—	—	—	~70
Bouillon, 1 cube	—	—	—	trace
Brazil nuts (see *Nuts*)				
Bread, 1 lb loaf:				
rye	—	—	—	trace
white, enriched, soft				
crumb type	3	8	2	trace
whole wheat, soft				
crumb type	2	6	2	trace
Broccoli, 10-oz frozen				
pkg., cooked	—	—	—	0
Brussels sprouts, 1 cup				
cooked	—	—	—	0
Butter:				
¼ lb (stick)	51	30	3	285.7
1 Tbs (⅛ stick)	6	4	trace	35.7
Cabbage, 1 cup raw or				
cooked	—	—	—	0
Cake, angelfood, 10-				
inch cake, unfrosted	—	—	—	0
Cake, baked from mix,				
made with eggs and				
milk, unfrosted	3	7	1	~125

Product	Saturated Fat (grams)	Mono-unsaturated (Oleic) Fatty Acid (grams)	Poly-unsaturated (Linoleic) Fatty Acid (grams)	Cholesterol (milligrams)
Candy:				
hard, 1 oz	—	—	—	0
milk chocolate, 1 oz	5	3	trace	0
Cantaloupe, ½ raw	—	—	—	0
Carrots, 1 cup raw or				
cooked	—	—	—	0
Cashew nuts (see *Nuts*)				
Cauliflower, 1 cup				
cooked	—	—	—	0
Celery, 1 cup raw	—	—	—	0
Cheeses:				
Cheddar	18	11	1	100
cottage, creamed	2	1	trace	15
cream	21	12	1	120
cheese spread and all				
other processed				
cheeses	15	9	1	85
Cherries, 1 cup canned	—	—	—	0
Chicken, raw:				
flesh only	2	2	1	60
skin only	5	6	3	60
Chickpeas (garbanzos)	trace	2	2	0
Chocolate:				
bitter or baking, 1 oz.	8	6	trace	trace
semi-sweet, 1 cup	34	22	1	trace
Clams, raw meat only	—	—	—	125+
Cocoa powder, with-				
out milk	1	1	trace	0
Coconut (see *Nuts*)				
Cola, 12 fl oz	—	—	—	0
Cookies, sandwich,				
chocolate or vanilla,				
commercial	1	1	trace	trace
Corn flakes, plain or				
sugar covered, 1 cup	—	—	—	0
Corn oil (see *Oils*)				
Corn, sweet, 1 ear	—	—	—	0
Cottonseed oil (see				
Oils)				

Product	Saturated Fat (grams)	Mono-unsaturated (Oleic) Fatty Acid (grams)	Poly-unsaturated (Linoleic) Fatty Acid (grams)	Cholesterol (milligrams)
Corned beef, boneless, cooked (medium fat)	15	13	1	70
Crabmeat	—	—	—	125
Crackers (see *Saltines* or *Graham*)				
Cranberry sauce, 1 cup canned	—	—	—	0
Cream:				
1 cup heavy	50	30	3	unknown but high
1 Tbs	3	2	trace	unknown but high
1 cup light	41	25	2	unknown but high
1 Tbs	3	2	trace	unknown but high
sour, 1 cup	26	16	1	unknown but high
Cucumber, 1 medium	—	—	—	0
Dates, 1 cup pitted	—	—	—	0
Egg, 1 large	2	3	trace	300
1 large white	—	—	—	0
1 large yolk	2	3	trace	300
Escarole, 2 oz	—	—	—	0
Figs, 1 large dried	—	—	—	0
Filberts (see *Nuts*)				
French dressing (see *Salad Dressing*)				
Fruit cocktail, 1 cup canned in heavy syrup	—	—	—	0
Fruit-flavored sodas, 12 fl oz	—	—	—	0
Gelatin:				
dessert powder, 3-oz pkg	—	—	—	0
unflavored dry powder, 1 envelope (1 Tbs)	—	—	—	0
Gin, 1½ fl oz	—	—	—	0

Product	Saturated Fat (grams)	Mono-unsaturated (Oleic) Fatty Acid (grams)	Poly-unsaturated (Linoleic) Fatty Acid (grams)	Cholesterol (milligrams)
Ginger ale, 12 fl oz	—	—	—	0
Graham crackers, 4 crackers	—	—	—	0
Grapefruit, 1 cup fresh or canned	—	—	—	0
Grapefruit juice, 1 cup fresh, frozen, or canned	—	—	—	0
Grapes, 1 cup raw	—	—	—	0
Grape juice, 1 cup canned, bottled or frozen	—	—	—	0
Ham, light cure, commercial	8	10	2	70
Hickory nuts (see *Nuts*)				
Honey, 1 Tbs.	—	—	—	0
Ice Cream:				
regular (~ 12% fat)	7	4	trace	45
rich (~ 16% fat)	12	7	1	45
ice milk	3	2	trace	unknown, but less than 45
Jams and preserves, 1 Tbs	—	—	—	0
Jellies, 1 Tbs	—	—	—	0
Lamb, raw:				
leg, untrimmed	9	6	trace	70
well trimmed	3	2	trace	70
rib, 1 chop,				
untrimmed	17	11	1	70
well trimmed	5	3	trace	70
shoulder, untrimmed	13	9	1	70
well trimmed	4	3	trace	70
Lard	38	46	10	95
Lemon, 1 raw	—	—	—	0
Lemon juice, 1 cup	—	—	—	0
Lemonade concentrate, 1 6-oz can	—	—	—	0
Lettuce, raw:				
Boston, 1 head	—	—	—	0
iceberg, 1 head	—	—	—	0

Product	Saturated Fat (grams)	Mono-unsaturated (Oleic) Fatty Acid (grams)	Poly-unsaturated (Linoleic) Fatty Acid (grams)	Cholesterol (milligrams)
Romaine, 2 large leaves	—	—	—	0
Lime, 1 raw	—	—	—	0
Lime juice, 1 cup	—	—	—	0
Lime concentrate, 1 6-oz can	—	—	—	0
Liver, beef, 2 oz fried	—	—	—	171.3
Macaroni, 1 cup cooked	—	—	—	0
Margarine:				
diet, ¼ lb (half tub)	8.5	17.1	19.8	0
hydrogenated vegetable oil				
¼ lb (one stick)	20.5	53.7	16	0
1 Tbs	2.5	6.7	2	0
liquid corn or other vegetable oil				
¼ lb (one stick)	21.7	35.4	33.1	0
1 Tbs	2.7	4.8	4.1	0
Marshmallows, 1 oz	—	—	—	0
Mayonnaise (see *Salad Dressing*)				
Milk, fluid, 1 8-oz glass:				
nonfat (skim)	—	—	—	6.7
whole (3.5% fat)	5	3	trace	26.5
Mushrooms, 1 cup fresh or canned	—	—	—	0
Noodles, 1 cup cooked	1	1	trace	trace
Nuts, shelled:				
almonds	4	36	11	0
beechnuts	4	27	16	0
Brazil nuts	13	32	17	0
cashew nuts	8	32	3	0
coconut, fresh	30	2	trace	0
coconut, dried, unsweetened	56	5	trace	0
filberts (hazelnuts)	3	34	10	0
hickory nuts	6	47	12	0
peanuts, raw	10	20	14	0

Product	Saturated Fat (grams)	Mono-unsaturated (Oleic) Fatty Acid (grams)	Poly-unsaturated (Linoleic) Fatty Acid (grams)	Cholesterol (milligrams)
peanuts, roasted	11	21	14	0
pecans	5	45	14	0
pistachios	5	35	10	0
walnuts, black	4	21	28	0
walnuts, English	4	10	40	0
Oatmeal, cooked, 1 cup	—	—	1	0
Ocean perch	—	—	—	~70
Okra, 8 pods cooked	—	—	—	0
Oils:				
corn				
1 cup	22	62	117	0
1 Tbs	1	4	7	0
cottonseed				
1 cup	55	46	110	0
1 Tbs	4	3	7	0
olive				
1 cup	24	167	15	0
1 Tbs	1	11	1	0
peanut				
1 cup	40	103	64	0
1 Tbs	3	7	4	0
safflower				
1 cup	18	37	165	0
1 Tbs	1	2	10	0
sesame seed				
1 cup	32	86.9	98.8	0
1 Tbs	2	5.4	6.1	0
soybean				
1 cup	33	44	114	0
1 Tbs	2	3	7	0
Olives:				
black, 3 small or 2 large	trace	2	trace	0
green, 4 medium or 3 extra large	trace	2	trace	0
Onions:				
raw, 1 onion	—	—	—	0
young green (6 scallions)	—	—	—	0

Product	Saturated Fat (grams)	Mono-unsaturated (Oleic) Fatty Acid (grams)	Poly-unsaturated (Linoleic) Fatty Acid (grams)	Cholesterol (milligrams)
Oranges, 1 medium	—	—	—	0
Orange juice, 1 cup fresh, canned, or frozen	—	—	—	0
Oysters	—	—	—	200
Papayas, 1 cup raw	—	—	—	0
Parsley, 1 Tbs raw	—	—	—	0
Peaches, 1 cup raw or canned	—	—	—	0
Peanuts (see *Nuts*)				
Peanut butter, 1 Tbs	2	4	2	trace
Peanut oil (see *Oils*)				
Pears, 1 cup raw or canned	—	—	—	0
Peas, green, 1 cup fresh or canned	—	—	—	0
Pecans (see *Nuts*)				
Peppers:				
hot, red (ground chili powder), 1 Tbs	—	—	—	0
sweet green, raw or cooked, 1 pepper	—	—	—	0
Pickles:				
dills, 1 medium	—	—	—	0
sweet gherkin, 1 medium	—	—	—	0
Pineapple, 1 cup raw or canned	—	—	—	0
Pineapple juice, 1 cup	—	—	—	0
Pistachio (see *Nuts*)				
Plums, 1 cup raw or canned	—	—	—	0
Pork:				
chop, 1 chop	8	9	2	70
loin, 3½ oz.	9	10	2	70
picnic, 3½ oz.	9	10	2	70
Potatoes, 1 medium baked or boiled	—	—	—	0
French fried in				

Product	Saturated Fat (grams)	Mono-unsaturated (Oleic) Fatty Acid (grams)	Poly-unsaturated (Linoleic) Fatty Acid (grams)	Cholesterol (milligrams)
cottonseed oil, 10 pieces, each 2x½x½ in.	2	2	4	0
Potato chips, 10 2-inch diameter	2	2	4	0
Pretzels, 1 thin twisted	—	—	—	0
Prunes, 1 cup dried, raw, or cooked	—	—	—	0
Prune juice, 1 cup	—	—	—	0
Pudding mix, dry form, 4-oz package	1	1	trace	0
Radishes, 4 raw	—	—	—	0
Raisins, 1 cup seedless	—	—	—	0
Raspberries, 1 cup raw or frozen	—	—	—	0
Rhubarb, 1 cup cooked	—	—	—	0
Rice, 1 cup puffed	—	—	—	0
Rice, 1 cup white, enriched, raw	—	—	—	0
Rum, 1½ fl oz	—	—	—	0
Safflower oil (see *Oils*)				
Safflower seed kernels, dry, hulled	5	9	43	0
Salad dressings, 1 Tbs commercial:				
French	1	1	3	0
mayonnaise	2	2	6	trace
thousand island	1	2	4	trace
Salmon, pink, raw	1	1	trace	~70
Salt pork, raw	32	39	5	90
Saltine crackers	3	7	1	0
Sauerkraut, 1 cup	—	—	—	0
Sausage and luncheon meats:				
spiced or unspiced, canned	9	11	2	70
pork links, raw	18	21	5	70
Sesame seeds, dry, whole	7	19	21	0
Shad	—	—	—	~70
Sherbet, 1 cup	—	—	—	0

Product	Saturated Fat (grams)	Mono-unsaturated (Oleic) Fatty Acid (grams)	Poly-unsaturated (Linoleic) Fatty Acid (grams)	Cholesterol (milligrams)
Shrimp	—	—	—	125
Soups:				
canned, 1 cup condensed, ready-to-serve, prepared with equal volume of milk				
cream of mushroom	4	4	5	13.5+
cream of tomato	3	2	1	13.5+
Dehydrated dry form:				
Onion mix (1½-oz pkg)	1	2	1	0
Soybean oil (see *Oils*)				
Soybeans, immature seeds, raw shelled	1	1	3	0
Spaghetti, 1 cup cooked	—	—	—	0
Spinach, 1 cup raw or cooked	—	—	—	0
Squash, 1 cup cooked:				
summer (yellow)	—	—	—	0
winter (acorn)	—	—	—	0
Strawberries, 1 cup raw or frozen	—	—	—	0
Sugars:				
brown, 1 cup	—	—	—	0
white, granulated or powdered, 1 cup	—	—	—	0
Sunflower seed kernels, dry, hulled	6	9	30	0
Sweet potatoes, fresh or canned	—	—	—	0
Tangerines, 1 raw	—	—	—	0
Tapioca, 1 cup dry	—	—	—	0
Tartar sauce, 1 Tbs.	1	1	4	trace
Tomatoes, fresh or canned	—	—	—	0
Tomato juice, 1 cup	—	—	—	0
Trout, raw rainbow	3	2	trace	~70
Tuna, canned in oil:				
drained	3	2	2	~70

Product	Saturated Fat (grams)	Mono-unsaturated (Oleic) Fatty Acid (grams)	Poly-unsaturated (Linoleic) Fatty Acid (grams)	Cholesterol (milligrams)
undrained	5	4	8	~70
Turnips, 1 cup cooked	—	—	—	0
Turkey:				
flesh only, raw	2	3	1	60
skin only, raw	11	17	8	60
Veal, medium fat, raw:				
chuck	5	4	trace	90
rib	7	6	trace	90
Vinegar, 1 Tbs	—	—	—	0
Vodka, 1½ fl oz	—	—	—	0
Walnuts, black (see *Nuts*)				
Watermelon, 1 wedge raw	—	—	—	0
Wheat germ, added nutrients, toasted	2	3	6	0
Whisky, 1½ fl oz	—	—	—	0
Wine	—	—	—	0
Yeast, 1 pkg dry active	—	—	—	0
Yogurt, 1 cup:				
made with partially skimmed milk	2	1	trace	6.7+
made from whole milk	5	3	trace	26.5+

About the Authors...

Elizabeth S. Weiss has a bachelor's degree from Skidmore College and a master's degree from Boston University. A native of Rochester New York who now lives in New York City, she has traveled extensively in Russia, Africa, and many other countries, collecting recipes along the way. A former editor at a major publishing company, she is a graduate of the Cordon Bleu Cooking School. Mrs. Weiss is married to a physician who is a firm believer in low cholesterol foods—especially delicious, gourmet low cholesterol foods.

Rita Parsont Wolfson, author of *The Penny-Pincher's Cookbook* and *The One-Pot Cookbook,* holds a bachelor's degree from Syracuse University, a master's degree from New York University, and has studied international cuisines at the Cordon Bleu Cooking School and the China Institute. She has collected many regional recipes during her travels through the United States, Canada, Europe, the Middle East, Africa, and Latin America, a number of which she has adapted to a low cholesterol eating plan. Mrs. Wolfson lives in Manhattan with her husband, an attorney. They own a large Samoyed who takes care of any leftovers.

Index

1 2 3 4 5 6 7 ← P Y → 9 8 7 6 5 4 3